HERE OR THERE

Table of Contents

Here or There 1

The Master Cup 8

Restoring the Exclamation Point 17

How Does the Midwest Sell Us on Winter 22

It took me 27 years to try a Big Mac 30

Hitting your Happiness Deductible 38

Those Times I Guarded a Chubby Draymond Green 44

My Sunday Affair at the Catholic Church 50

Forgive me, Baseball 56

Just an Old Guy at a Pizza Place 62

The 36-hour Car Alarm 70

The Lost Art of Complaining 75

Will Alexa Fall in Love? 82

Embarrassment is the Emotional Terrorist 90

I'll Always Cheer For Wile E. Coyote 98

Relaxed People Stress me Out 104

Virginia Woolf Kicked the Crap out of Me 110

Farewell, LOL 116

The Escalator Dictator 124

But Maybe "Living in the Moment" Is Overrated 130

Winter is About Lowering Your Expectations 140

How to Avoid Playing on The Work League Softball Team 147

Check Your Font Size, Bro 152

Dinner for One 161

I'm Good with Whatever..167

I Heard That Was Disappointing..173

What was the Worst Part of Your Trip? 179

Guilt is Good..185

Sometimes You Hop in The Car with a Stranger 191

Moral Dilemma in the Laundry Room 197

Celebrate BEFORE the Signature...203

What's Your Name Again?...208

Big Decisions are Overrated 214

Acknowledgements

About Long Overdue Books + Upcoming Projects

There is a time for everything,
And a season for every activity under the heavens:
A time to be born and a time to die,
A time to plant and a time to uproot,
A time to kill and a time to heal,
A time to tear down and a time to build,
A time to weep and a time to laugh,
A time to mourn and a time to dance,
Ecclesiastes 3

I would not like them Here or There.
I would not like them anywhere.

I do not like green eggs and ham.
I do not like them, Sam-I-am
Dr. Seuss

When in Rome, do as you done in Milledgeville.
Flannery O'Connor

If only we'd stop trying to be happy, we'd have a pretty good time.
Edith Wharton

I am not afraid of death,
I just don't want to be there when it happens.
Woody Allen

We're all just one stitch away from Here to There.
Wheezy, *Toy Story 2*

The only thing to do with good advice is to pass it on.
It is never of any use to oneself.
Oscar Wilde

I can only note that the past is beautiful because one never realizes an emotion at the time. It expands later, and thus we don't have complete emotions about the present, only about the past.
Virginia Woolf

If you laugh, you think, and you cry, that's a full day.
That's a heck of a day.
You do that seven days a week, you're going
to have something special.
Jim Valvano

You can walk the streets of Florence a thousand times but it will always be like the first time. You'll discover a Florence at six in the morning, and one at eight. There will be a Florence of ten and one at noon. And another Florence at two and one at five in
the late afternoon.
Fabio Picchi

Sweet are the uses of adversity,
Which like the toad, ugly and venomous,
Wears yet a precious jewel in his head
As You Like It

If it's good bread, it don't need any butter.
And if it ain't good bread, then why are you eating it?
Guy who Camped Next to us at High School Senior Skip

For anyone going through a hard time,
Who wishes things would get better.
Or for anyone going through a great time,
Who wishes it would last forever.

Or for anyone who reads this poem and thinks
"Hey man, this is kind of corny."
Whoever you are, wherever you are,
This might be the book for you.

Chapter 1

Here or There

Have you ever run into someone right after a vacation who didn't realize you had ever left?

This happened to me the other day. I ran into a colleague who I hadn't seen in over a month. We dived into the standard Midwestern: *"Hey, how are ya? How ya been?"* but instead of responding with the regular, "Good, good," I replied that I was jet-lagged.

Oh yeah? Did you go on a trip?

Yep. Just got back from Italy.

For two-and-a-half weeks, my wife and I were 5,000+ miles away, traveling from Rome to Florence to Cinque Terre. And, for as far away from Chicago as I felt that we were, I realized—at least to this co-worker—my absence was no different than had I been in one of the other office buildings. They were Here. I was There.

After we walked our separate ways, I had the same dazed look on my face as a college freshman who just heard the universe is still expanding. I thought to myself, "There are really only two places in the world: Here or There."

Woah...

The reality is we spend most of our time Here, but we love There. Just listen to the way people say Here. It's always aggressive and desperate. *I'm dyin' here! Get me outta here!* There's an exhaustion with Here. *Oh, here we go again. Here, just listen to me.*

How about the world's most famous and effective pickup line: *Hey, let's get out of here.* Why does it work? Because everyone wants to get out of a Here. Or listen to the lady down the street pleading to her dog: *"Here, boy, here. Here!"* We're begging because even a dog doesn't want to come to a Here.

Compare it to There. *"Hey, whatcha guys doing over there?" "What's going on over there?" "Look, over there!"* There's hope. There's mystery. There's even comfort. *There, there, everything's gonna be alright.*

A There is inspiring. How did we rally millions of Americans to fight in a giant war? Start the music: *"Over THERE! Over THERE!"* People instinctively started marching.

When somebody uses the cliché, "It's neither here nor there," I couldn't disagree more. It's ONLY Here or There. That's it! There are no other options. The wisest person in the world is the operator who answers the phone, and when you ask, "Is Robert in today?" they reply, "Nope. He's not Here." They don't have to say where he is. Don't have to distinguish if he's on a trip, if he's sick, or if he's out playing golf. He's just. Not. Here.

But we can't get enough of There. So, we travel. We go all around the world. Then we come back Here and sit at a table with a group of friends and talk about our favorite trips. We were in Italy. *Oh my gosh, I wanna go to Italy so bad.* We were in Japan. *Oh, I'd love to see Japan.* We did two weeks in Paris. *Oh, Paris, that's on our bucket list for sure.*

I would argue there is no difference between these destinations to someone who is Here. It's just a different There. Eat new food. See new things. Meet new people. But, at its core, the trip is fun because you've escaped a Here. You could get the same thrill by taking a sick day. Or going to an appointment. Like, have you ever taken a random Wednesday off of work? You're the happiest person in the world. And all you did was go to the dentist! But you broke the routine. Switched things up from a Here to a There. And it didn't cost thousands of dollars.

There is also this assumption that people over There have it better than us. *Could you imagine living over There?* But, to them, it's a Here. Nobody over there is saying, "What do you wanna do tonight?" "Oh, I dunno, I figured I'd go stare at the Colosseum for a couple of hours, just really take it in."

No, they probably sit down on a couch and watch Netflix. Or pull out their phones. Or say, "Man, there's nothing to do around Here."

Because that's what you do when it's a Here. On our trip, I saw plenty of Italians wearing New York Yankees hats or Los Angeles Lakers t-shirts. One guy was rocking an old Chicago Bulls jersey. To them, we are their elusive There. They fantasize about going to an exotic place in the United States. They sit down, look at a map, and say, "Ah, if only I could go and visit the Midwest. I just wanna see Illinois."

No matter where you are in the world, every location has its regular mundane moments of Here.

So yes, there's amazing homemade pizza in Italy, but there's also a guy eating a thing of pizza flavored Pringles.

Yes, the sites are incredible, but there's also a girl sitting behind the counter looking at Pokémon Go.

And yes, it was the most relaxing few weeks of me and Ashley's life, but in one of our most serene moments of There, we saw a family of four sitting at a table next to us going through a universal Here moment.

The teenage daughter had her arms crossed in front of her chest. The mom took away her phone. The teenager yelled and started to cry. The dad said something in Italian that I couldn't understand, but was pretty sure it translated to, "Hey, don't talk to your mother that way." The younger sister chimed in, antagonizing the older sister the same way a younger sibling would in Chicago, in Paris, in Tokyo, and yes, in Italy too.

To us, we were in paradise. To them, it was anything but.

There is no guarantee you can always escape from a Here; even on vacation. Even thousands of miles away from home. Here or There are as much physical places as they are a mindset.

It all starts before the trip with any of your friends who have been to the same There. The first thing they do: make a list. *Oh, you've gotta go here, and here, and here.* There is so much pressure to see the same sites, do what they did, you run the risk of duplicating their entire trip. This is why so many people who visit New York City come back with the same stories about seeing the Statue of Liberty, Times Square, and the Brooklyn Bridge. Same thing in Rome with the Colosseum, Trevi Fountain, and The Pantheon. But, if you don't see those things, there's too much guilt. You went all the way over THERE and didn't see/do/experience this??

So, you compile your lists from friends and family. Lists from Tripadvisor. Lists from Rick Steves. *Here. Here. Here.* You pack your suitcases. You're ready to go. You're heading out of the office when someone asks, not even asks, but *confirms* you'll be posting your stories on Facebook. Instagram. Snapchat. Not after your trip is finished, but during. You must document your There in real time.

You get on the plane. Land. Hop in the taxi. After the jetlag wears off, there's this new, unfamiliar feeling that starts to take over your body. All of the stress, all of the deadlines, all of the day-to-day grind is gone. You have no alarm clocks. No agenda. No responsibilities. The feeling of a There has now settled deep into your bones. *Wait, is this... pure joy? Is this what it feels like to be... relaxed?*

But Here is never far away. It whispers through your phone. *Pssst, over here. Yeah, come here for a second. Check your emails. Here, check your texts. Give Instagram a few scrolls, will ya? It won't hurt.*

In Italy, I tried to keep the Here out of my There, and I'm happy to say I only lost a couple of times. For most of the trip, I was off the grid. Living in the moment. Like the time we were walking around St. Mark's Square in Venice. I had a fresh calzone in hand and was staring off in the distance at the bell tower when out of nowhere a massive seagull—who could've won any arm-wrestling contest— swooped in, plucked the calzone right out of my hand. He landed ten feet away and, in seconds, twenty other seagulls joined him, completely devouring my lunch. Not a crumb left behind. Ashley burst into laughter. I was still in shellshock; like a little kid losing an ice cream cone. *"Hey, that was mine."* A year later, 10 years later, when we're telling friends about our time over There, the Venice story isn't complete without the great calzone heist of St. Mark's Square.

Or the first night we were in Florence walking down Via dei Calzaiuoli, a street name you don't really find around Here. Ashley and I were walking hand in hand passing by all of these cool little shops. And everything smells incredible in Florence. Back home, I don't even have a sense of smell. Just a Midwestern stuffy nose. But over There, I've got the nose of a sommelier or like the co-worker who's always first to notice a subtle fart.

We looked to our right and there was the Cathedral of Santa Maria del Fiore. Somehow this massive, beautiful, almost 600-year-old church sneaks up on you. Immediately puts you at a loss for words. I had an English professor who used to say, "When you become a writer, you officially give up the right to use the expression, 'Words can't describe this,'" but when you're looking up at the front of the cathedral or, even more so, the Duomo behind it, I don't know what else there is to say. Maybe this is the feeling we should aim for; to be so consumed by There, that there aren't any words for it.

And of course, a few moments later, I reached for the iPhone. Started taking photos and videos and selfies like everyone else in front of the old Cathedral. But for that brief moment, craning my neck, looking up at those two masterpieces, I was completely There.

Did I need to go 5,000 miles away to have this type of moment? I joked that it's no different than taking a random Wednesday off of work, but that's not true at all. It was a hundred times better. And the sites were part of it. The food helped. The wine helped too.

But maybe, just as much of a factor as all of the things above was the decision to be fully There. Accepting that Here could wait.

And the more I thought about it, the more I continue to think about it, the more I'm convinced that if there are only two places in the world—Here or There—we should go ahead and experience the one where we're at.

Work Life Balance

Chapter 2

The Master Cup

Growing up in the '90s, every home in America had at least one Master Cup. The Master Cup stood anywhere from one to two feet tall and could hold an absurd amount of liquid. It kept ice tray manufactures in business and absolutely thrived on Saturday and Sunday afternoons.

When you were at a friend's house playing video games, their mom would come in and say, "Help yourself to the kitchen; we've got milk, water, some pops out in the garage." You'd get up and navigate through their unfamiliar cabinets trying to find the cups.

Plates. Nope. Spice rack. Nope. Ah ha, there they are.

On one side were the glasses. Half short, half tall. The glasses were clear and breakable, which didn't bode well for my greasy fingers. Next to the glasses, sometimes on a different shelf altogether, were the cups. Cups in the '90s were plastic and perfect for my pizza roll fingers. They were always big and colorful; like shirts on *Saved by the Bell* or *The Fresh Prince of Bel Air*. The art ranged from university logos to Looney Tunes characters.

And there, in a row all by itself, was The Master Cup.

Some families installed a spotlight over theirs, others put it behind a layer of glass like it were a museum exhibit. This was off limits.

Take it off the shelf, and you were riding your bike home, permanently banned from ever coming back. The Master Cup was reserved for your friend's dad who would come in like a giant, scratching his belly—*hey kids, scuse me*—grabs the cup, empties an entire ice tray and puts it under the faucet.

No matter where you were in the country, you had a version of The Master Cup. In Michigan, eight out of ten households had a Master Cup with a faded photo of Barry Sanders breaking a tackle. In Chicago, it was the Bulls starting five. New York had a faded image of Derek Jeter and the '98 Yankees. Even if you weren't a sports family, you still had a Master Cup in the cabinet; usually from McDonald's, Taco Bell, or the largest Big Gulp size available from 7-11.

Filling up Master Cup meant the rest of the day was going to involve nothing but the couch and the bathroom; which was perfect in the Midwest where half of the year is spent hiding from the winter. In terms of size, these cups held anywhere from 48 to 148 fluid ounces. You could dump an entire two liter of soda in there without fear of an overflow. Fill it up with a carton of milk, and you had enough dairy to dip through an entire box of Oreos or Chips Ahoy.

But Master Cup was always at its best with ice water. And remember, this was the late '90's, so Brita filters were still pretty much science fiction and sparkling water was only available in France. However, with Master Cup, there was no need to run the water through any sort of filter. No need to add any flavor. You'd go straight from the faucet. Straight from a hose out back. No matter what the source, that water always became the coldest, purest water you'd ever tasted; which made no sense because the Master Cup alternated between pop, milk, and tap water without any sort of dish soap in between.

The Master Cup was a rite of passage. Sometime between your 11th birthday and getting your driver's license, your dad came home with a Super-Sized cup from McDonald's, ran it under the faucet, handed it over. *My child, you are ready.* And the cup still smelled like Diet Coke, but you took that first sip, and it was glorious. It was everything you ever hoped for, and you longed for the day when you would graduate from the McDonald's training wheels to a true Master Cup of your own.

Then something happened...

Life went on. I graduated high school, went to college, got married, and one Bed Bath & Beyond registry later, our cabinets looked like the ones I remember from childhood. Nice breakable glasses on one side, plastic cups on the other. And an absurd amount of coffee mugs.

But there was no Master Cup...

I don't remember the exact date, but there was a cold Saturday morning when I went into the kitchen, grabbed a regular glass and decided, you know what, no, I don't want a glass, I want a cup. I want to sit down with a giant Master Cup and watch basketball with enough ice water to last me an entire weekend. I decided it was time to carve out some space on a shelf and go purchase my first official adult Master Cup. One that should carry me for the next 60 years.

I had no idea the journey I was about to embark on. This wasn't your '90's shopping mall with a whole row of Master Cups available in the front of a Target. I went to two or three stores and couldn't find anything. Their "cup" section was trying to do too much. Trying to be too sleek. None of the cups were even that big. It seemed like the goal was to save cabinet space, not devour entire ice trays.

These hybrid water bottle cups have over complicated things. Yes, I'm sure it's nice that the cup is dishwasher safe, doubles as a water bottle, and it's eco-friendly, gluten-free, whatever else, but they are missing the main point of a Master Cup. Convenience was never Master Cup's selling point. It didn't matter that it was awkward to find shelf space, or that it would explode in the dishwasher, no, Master Cup knew how to do one thing and one thing right: hold a lot of liquid.

That's it. Simple. There didn't need to be anything else.

But now you can't find one anywhere.

I left the mall with so many questions. *When did the Master Cups disappear? Why did it happen? Who killed The Master Cup?*

The first suspect: former New York City Mayor Michael Bloomberg. He made any location that sold Master Cups feel like they were part of a drug cartel. Don't quote me on this, but I believe you could get 25-to-life for selling a Master Cup in Manhattan.

Forget that the Master Cup was at its best with ice water, the perception was—and still is—that it serves as a sugary drink trafficker. And I know trends can change, but it feels like the anti-sugar movement is here to stay. The push for a healthy lifestyle keeps getting stronger and stronger. Just look at the clothing. In the '90s, the emphasis was on everything baggy; big shirts, big pants. There was room to hide a few love handles. Now it's all "athleisure." Yoga pants. Slim fit shirts. Everyone in Chicago looks like they're either headed to a yoga class or training for the next triathlon.

Health is one concern, and once you pair that with the Master Cup's perceived negative impact on the environment, it's impossible to survive both of these passionate groups coming at you all at once. But, again, I think the environmental impact is also an unfair allegation. If the concern is plastic cups will end up in landfills or float around in the ocean, I will counter with the fact that a Master Cup's literal shelf life is north of 35 years. Every '85 Chicago Bears Master Cup is still in use and Master Cup Barry Sanders never retired. You could spend years digging through a landfill without finding a single Master Cup.

Because, if Master Cup was ever chipped, cracked, accidentally sat on, that wasn't the end. Not at all. You got out the duct tape, or just accepted that it was going to drip a little bit on the couch. Under no circumstance should Master Cup EVER go in the trash. Relationships have ended over much smaller offenses.

Especially now that the Master Cup is facing extinction. I am worried that our grandkids will never experience what it's like to have a lazy weekend day with the remote control in one hand and a Master Cup in the other. I am saddened every time I see someone reach for another Oreo but not have enough milk left for the dunk. I feel sorry for modern sports stars like Draymond Green or Mike Trout who will never know what it's like to be immortalized on a giant plastic cup.

Look. Now is not the time to point my pizza roll finger. It doesn't matter how we got here, who's responsible, or who's to blame for the last twenty years of Master Cup decline. What matters now is that we act and we act quickly.

It's time to bring back The Master Cup.

Proven Science:
The more ice trays you have,
the less actual cubes

CHAPTER 3

Restoring the Exclamation Point

I love the exclamation point. When you see a "!" it even looks like it's yelling at you. Just like the period says, "We're done here," the comma says, "Hey, take a breath," and the question mark looks like someone is lost asking for directions, the exclamation point—at least at one point in time—had a clear purpose; it meant that someone was either angry or excited.

It would look weird to write a line of dialogue where someone is shouting and end it with a period. You need the exclamation point to pack a punch.

But where it doesn't need to show up is in about every email I send. For example, here's what a typical email of mine looks like:

> Hey Name!
>
> Happy Friday! Just looked over the whatever and it looks good to go. Could you do the work thing and the other work thing?
>
> Thanks!

Three out of five sentences ended with an exclamation point. Why am I yelling? My tone is like a high school cheerleader. *When I say, "Go!" you say, "Fight!" Go! Fight! Go! Fight!*

And what I'm doing isn't uncommon. I'm writing in standard Millennial email-ese. The person receiving the email understands the exclamation points are friendly placeholders, not to be taken seriously.

The person who gets screwed over in all of this is the one who writes emails without these friendly, yet meaningless, exclamation points. Look at the same exact email with the exclamation points swapped out with periods:

Hey Name.
Happy Friday, I guess. Just looked over the whatever and it looks good enough, you dirtbag. Could you do the work thing and the other work thing, preferably while we're both still young? I hate you. I seriously hate you.
Thanks for nothing.

As you can see, all I did was take out the exclamation points, and it went from friendly to, "What's their problem?" Could be the nicest person in the office, but now they're established as an email jerk.

The email and text message markets are oversaturated with exclamation points. They carry little to no value anymore. Since one exclamation point is always expected, moments like "Happy Birthday!!" or "Thank you!!!" now need two or three to demonstrate the true level of excitement.

The solution? I think we need to put exclamation points in Swiss bank accounts. Take millions of these out of circulation for a while and try to regain some of their original value. I mean look at the incredibly rare semi-colon; any time I see one of those things, it's like spotting a two-dollar bill. Granted, I don't really know what to do with it, not sure how it differs from a comma, but it's always exciting to see one out in the wild.

Once the exclamation point regains its full value, we'll start to appreciate exclamation points the way the Spanish language does by throwing in an upside down one (¡) at the beginning of a sentence. In the office, we'll see someone's face turn red, see them grab the keyboard, and we'll all gather around their desk. *"Dude, can you BCC me on that email?"*

So, how do we fix this? What can we do as early as tomorrow to solve this growing epidemic?

One Medium Rare solution is at the end of an email, where we normally put, "Thanks!" to go with "Thanks," and that way the "thanks + comma" doubles as a "Sincerely," then throw in your signature underneath. It's a simple but very effective move.

Or maybe we need to come up with a different punctuation point to serve as a milder exclamation point. We could introduce a new symbol or give new purpose to an old dusty one. Look at the jolt of life "#" received as a hashtag after decades of being the boring pound sign. Maybe we could rebrand this guy ~ or start throwing in the {squiggly parenthesis}.

I say we find the halfway point. We cut the exclamation point in half, drop the floating line, and keep the period. See, problem solved!

Sorry, old habits die hard.

Let me try again:

Problem solved.

I trust my gut, but it doesn't always trust me

"Not the cheese balls again!!!"

CHAPTER 4

How Does the Midwest Sell Us on Winter

Let's say money is not an issue. And you could move anywhere in the country. Anywhere in the world. You could wake up every day in Italy or never see snow again down in the Bahamas. You could go to places where the temperature is just the temperature; there's no "feels like negative 15." Go to a place where it always "feels like" a good day for the beach.

Where would you go?

For me, even if I had unlimited options, unlimited Theres to choose from, I know I would ultimately stay here in the Midwest. I can say with almost one hundred percent certainty that I will spend the rest of my days here in Chicago (or maybe Northern Michigan).

And I know, I know, people might say, "Well, you never know where life will take you" or "There could be an exciting opportunity somewhere else. Nobody really knows their future."

But I'm pretty sure about mine. At least location wise.

The reason for this unbridled confidence? It's simple: the Midwest is phenomenal at sales. To use an old cliché, they say the best salesperson "can sell ice to an Eskimo." Well, Chicago, Michigan, Ohio,

Iowa, Kansas, Missouri, they achieve this feat every single year. The Midwest has somehow convinced us that seven-month winters are actually a *good* thing.

Here's how it works. The Midwest sales and marketing teams slowly walk into the conference room. It's the heart of January, everyone on the team feels dejected. Hopeless. They're all wearing winter jackets indoors. One person is wrapped up in a blanket. Everyone can see their own breath.

They hear laughter down the hall from the California and Florida conference rooms. For those teams, every day of the week is casual Friday.

"Oh, oh!" someone from the Florida/California room says in a loud, excited voice. "We could start with a shot of the golf course, then pan out to the wineries and people on the beach and a couple holding hands riding horseback and somebody surfing and snorkeling and then more smiling families. Close with a beautiful sunset. We could get celebrities. Put in a Kardashian or two."

"That's it! Done! Everyone, take the rest of the day off. You know what, take the rest of the *week* off!"

The person in charge of the Midwest meeting is about to speak, about to rally the troops when someone at the table cuts them off.

"Look, we're screwed," she says. "How can we convince people to live in the Midwest? I mean just listen to what they're saying down the hall. Surfing? Napa Valley? Dip my toes in the ocean? We can't compete with that. I haven't even *felt* my toes since Thanksgiving! They've got sunshine; we haven't seen the sky in two weeks. It's over. You don't see Antarctica panicking because they don't have enough people. Siberia doesn't worry about their lack of tourism. Let's just accept what we are and move on. We're too cold."

"Look," the leader of the board says. "We can either give up, or we can work with what we've got. We need to stay positive. We need to be ready to fight. We need to take the gloves off!"

Everyone around the table starts to take off their mittens.

"I meant more of a metaphor; you know what, that's fine. Let's do this! Let's hear some ideas."

There's silence for a moment before a shy person near the door speaks up. He's looking at his feet the entire time.

"What if we somehow like, I dunno, said snow was, um, like a good thing?"

"Great! Alright, let's work with that."

"We could tell everyone how Christmas just isn't the same without snow."

"Perfect! More. More ideas!"

The woman who spoke out at the beginning, let's give her a good Midwestern name, "Catherine" rolls her eyes.

"Why would people be upset not to have snow on Christmas?" Catherine says. "I have a cousin in Miami who celebrates Christmas with a bar-b-q on the beach every single year. It sounds delightful."

"Oh, but it's not the same."

"So true. It's not the same."

"Not the same at all."

Catherine scrunches her eyebrows together.

"You're saying 'it's not the same' as if that were a *bad* thing?"

"Gotta have snow. Gotta have a white Christmas."

"Maybe we could have Bing Crosby sing a song about it, make a movie too? How does he feel about winter?"

"Mutual I'm sure," the leader says. "Jot that down. This is great, love the energy, love the vibes. But how do we market snow?"

"You could like roll it into a ball and throw it at your friends?"

"Great!"

"We could show people how to make these bigger balls of snow, and you could like stack them on top of each other. And then you could grab a carrot and some charcoal. Make a snowman. I feel like kids would love that."

"Ha, bigger balls," joke guy chimes in. The whole room snickers.

"We could have people lay down in the snow and do a jumping jack kind of thing. Call it a snow angel?"

"Who would do that??" Catherine says.

"Oh! I got one! This might be a little bit out there, but you know how they have water skiing in Florida? What if we did that, but on snow?"

"We don't have any mountains?" Catherine says.

"Eh, we'll use hills. Or maybe just a flat stretch of land, call it 'cross country skiing.'"

"That sounds miserable," Catherine says.

"No, not at all. I think it's a great idea. What else? What else?"

"We could go to a frozen lake, cut a hole in the ice, and go fishing?" *GREAT!*

"We could emphasize to parents how cute their kids look all bundled up in coats and hats?" *PERFECT!*

"We could fill up a hot tub with hot chocolate and sprinkle little marshmallows on top and tell people to hop in?" *HEY, LITTLE BIT WEIRD, BUT WHY NOT!*

Catherine can't take it anymore. She stands up and smacks her hand on the table.

"Enough! Look, this morning I woke up, I went to my car, I literally scraped ice off the windshield with my credit card. Every time my dog has to pee, I have to throw on my coat, my boots, my hat, my gloves. And this is our lives every single fricken year! Every year from November to what, March? April? May? You can't sell people on this. It's impossible!"

"So, then why have you stayed?" the shy person sitting by the door asks.

The room is silent until the conference phone buzzes. One of the remote employees has joined the call.

"Hey, it's Bill from Minnesota, sorry I'm late. My car wouldn't start."

"No worries, Bill. What's the weather like up there?"

"Oh man, we're looking at a balmy negative 12."

Everyone mouths the word 'wow.' The phone buzzes again.

"Hi everyone, Debbie in Wisconsin."

"Debbie! I heard you guys got pounded with snow last night? How much?"

"Eight inches."

"Wow!"

"Yeah, took me about an hour to dig out my car!"

Catherine looks around and sees a new level of camaraderie in the room. People are on the edge of their seats swapping winter war stories.

She wasn't sure why the memory came to mind, but she remembered way back in seventh grade sitting down at a cafeteria table, and these girls she never met before started sharing stories about their crappiest day or their most embarrassing moments. One girl shared the worst parts of her recent vacation. Until that moment, Catherine always thought you were supposed to be happy, all the time, that you never—under any circumstances—talk about the bad stuff. Just put on a smile and stay positive.

She remembered how finally it was her turn to share. She nervously shared her best-worst story, and they all laughed, together. There was comfort in the suckiness. The last person at the table chimed in, *"You know what, I've never really had that bad of a day before. Life's been pretty good to me."* Everyone at the table rolled their eyes.

The phone buzzes again.

"Hey, guys, Robert down in Del Rio, Texas. Sorry I wasn't here earlier. My kid's been sick this morning. Ah, who am I kidding, I was out playing golf. But hey, that's neither here nor there. So, corporate asked me to join your call, see if y'all needed help with ideas. Man, I looked at the weather map today, I hate to say it, but we're 100 degrees warmer down here. Isn't that something? Y'all should move down! Anyways, here's what I'm thinking. You should just focus on the summer months in your ad campaign. Hide the winter. Talk about how great June and July are up north. How you can go sailing, and—"

Catherine looked around the room. Everyone was rolling their eyes. One person was moving their hand like a little Pac-Man mouthing blah-blah-blah. She looked next to her and saw the lift ticket for Boyne Mountain hanging from the zipper of a colleague's coat. "Mountain," she thought to herself, shook her head, and smiled.

She was starting to have a Grinch's heart grew three sizes type of moment. She could see her middle school table again. She could picture Robert from Del Rio, Texas, pulling up a chair. *You know what, I've never really had that bad of a day before. Life's been pretty good to me.* She could feel the room turning against the fair-weather fan.

"Hey, Robert," Catherine said. "We're actually right in the middle of something here. Could you put yourself on mute?"

The candy cane is the most festive way to treat heartburn

CHAPTER 5

It took me 27 years to try a Big Mac

My Dad always ordered the Number 1 at McDonald's. Big Mac, fries, and a Diet Coke. I got the Happy Meal. He got the Meal of Respect. Mine came with a toy. His came with a nap. And a Super-Sized Master Cup.

He would bring the Big Mac box over to the table, and I would look in awe.

Say Pa, you think I could eat one of those someday?

"Someday, son. Someday."

Doesn't get more iconic than the Big Mac. *Two all-beef patties, special sauce, lettuce, cheese, pickles, onions on a sesame seed bun.* As a kid, I wasn't nearly ready. I was far too picky. I would have ordered it without lettuce. Without pickles. Without onions. And, at that point, it's really not a Big Mac at all.

Because a Big Mac is not meant to be modified. It'd be like asking for a Corvette with an automatic transmission or a Rocky marathon without *Rocky IV*. America's iconic burger is supposed to be displayed in all its glory; the toppings fresh from a garden in California, the cheese assembled from the happiest cows in Wisconsin, the tomatoes delivered fresh from Italy. When you're driving down the highway and see a Big Mac on a billboard, there's always a bright light shining behind it as if it came straight down from the heavens.

And remember the good old days when Super-Size was still an option? When the calorie count wasn't displayed on the box? Things have definitely changed since then and, as a result, the Big Mac has faced growing pressure from the health-conscious community. It puts the Big Mac in a precarious spot because—if McDonald's tries to appease the health and wellness crowd, and turns the three buns into a lettuce wrap—they run the risk of losing their most loyal supporters. The Tim Allen "More Power" crowd will move on to a bigger burger at a different fast food restaurant.

It's kind of like football. When football tries to make the game safer, enforcing penalties for breathing on the quarterback, it appeases the "football is not safe" group, but the die-hard fanbase is left complaining how things have gotten way too soft. The die-hards might turn away from football to more violent options like UFC or national politics.

The Big Mac can never be a salad, nor can it go toe-to-toe with the "Baconator" at Wendy's, or Burger King's "Big King," or whatever monster burger Hardee's rolls out there with a bikini-clad Paris Hilton taking a giant bite at a car wash.

But, oddly enough, the health community never doubles down on these newer heavier villains. Even when KFC released the "Double Down," an unprecedented sandwich that swapped out the buns with pieces of fried chicken, the Big Mac STILL had the largest target on its back. It's the dinosaur of the fast food industry that dietitians would love to see go extinct. It's sad, and I hate to put this thought out there but—just like the Master Cup—you have to wonder if the Big Mac will still be around for our grandkids to order...

I mean, look at what's happened to its spot on the menu. McDonald's still keeps it at Number 1, but it's kind of like when teams keep their aging Hall-of-Fame star in the starting lineup; the fans smile and clap, but everyone knows it's the Quarter Pounder's team now and secretly wishes the Double Quarter Pounder would be named as the new starting quarterback.

What I didn't realize, until recently, was just how far the Big Mac has fallen. A few months ago, I walked by a McDonald's and saw the sign, "Two Big Macs for $5." This can't be happening! I know McDonald's is making significant roster moves like the All-Day Breakfast and testing out menu options from all around the world, but this? *This?* They're sending the franchise player down to the can-I-get-a-McPick-2?! Sharing poster space with the Filet-o-Fish?

I wanted to help out, I really did, but I still don't like pickles, and I've got a weird thing against shredded lettuce. As a kid, we would go to Taco Bell and I'd order three tacos, no lettuce. Occasionally they would mess up, and my mom would actually pick off the small individual pieces of lettuce like a surgeon removing shards of glass. That's when you know what love is; when your mom is down in the weeds picking lettuce off a softshell taco.

So, with a heavy sigh, I went back to the tried and true chicken nuggets. I left the Big Mac in the McPick bargain bin. Off in the distance, I could hear the starstruck Filet-O-Fish asking the Big Mac for a selfie.

"Arrrgh, it's good to have ye here, matie."

Then something changed. I don't know if it was Trump's call to buy American or what, but I decided my Big Mac streak ends right here, right now. Twenty-seven years is too long to go without trying a Big Mac. If I needed to Peter Piper pick the pickles off the burger then fine, I'd do it at the table in shame, but I refuse to look the other way as this poor old Wooly Mammoth takes on any more spears.

But here's the problem: I was broke. I looked at my checking account and saw a tender $4.90. Not even a McPick 2 to my name. Worse, Ashley had the credit card. So, unless McDonald's would accept my Great Clips gift card as some new form of cliptocurrency, I didn't see how I could pull this off.

Now, obviously, the easy answer was to wait until tomorrow's payday, but I couldn't. I was too inspired.

So, I did what any desperate Millennial would do; I asked my buddy Jamen if he could Quickpay me three dollars. Get you back next week. Think of that; we live in a time where a friend can magically send you three dollars from South Carolina to Chicago just so you can get fries and a Coke.

With $7.90 to my name, I hopped on the bus heading north to McDonald's.

I felt a similar feeling on that Chicago bus as I did back in high school when we would travel to Saginaw to play future NBA star Draymond Green. It starts to sink in: *we don't stand a chance, do we?* Too big. Too strong. But there's no turning back. That game is coming, whether we like it or not. Soon I'd be lined up against the Big Mac.

I walked into McDonald's and saw advertisements for the Mac Jr. and the Grand Mac. A lot to digest here. One angle, this could be McDonald's way of saying eff you to the dietitians. *"You want us to take the Big Mac off the menu? Cool, how about we make two more instead!"* Or maybe, back to the football point, the smaller Mac Jr. is to appease the health concerns and the Grand Mac is to challenge their UFC opponents. *"Grand Mac vs. The Baconator - Battle of the Belt Buckle."* Kill two birds with one kidney stone.

I approached the counter, studied the prices to see if there was any way I could still squeeze a McFlurry into the order.

"Yeah, can I get a Number 1," I said casually as if this was a typical, everyday order for me. I didn't want to show any signs of my Big Mac virginity.

The order came out to be $7.24. *Whew.* Cleared the bar by sixty-six cents.

Bad news: Not enough for a McFlurry. Good news: I didn't go bankrupt at a McDonald's.

I was confused by the total price. I know there was fries and a Coke, but it still seemed weird to me. I thought I could get a Big Mac AND a Filet-o-Fish for five dollars. How come Big Mac + fries + drink is that much more? Does anyone know what a Filet-o-Fish costs? Does it cost anything at all?

Customer: How much is a Big Mac?

Clerk: Five dollars

Customer: Then what's a Big Mac plus a Filet-o-Fish?

Clerk: Right around five dollars.

Customer: (scratches head) Wait, so, hang on a second, is the Filet-o-Fish... *free?*

Clerk: Yeah, we just kind of hand those things out to anyone who asks. It's all funded by the Catholic church.

In terms of pickiness, I stuck to the original plan, ordered the Big Mac with no modifications. Opened the box and there it was. Not as big as I remember from my Dad's orders growing up, but it's still a beast. A big beautiful sandwich. I debated picking off the lettuce and pickles but thought, you know what, sometimes in life, you just gotta gut it out.

First bite: awesome. I've heard rumors that the special sauce is just thousand island dressing. I don't think that's the case. Whatever it is, it's better than ketchup and mustard, mayo, or bbq sauce on a burger. Bite two: I hit the first big patch of shredded lettuce. *Oof.* I wasn't going to pick it off or call in my mom from the bullpen but, thankfully, some of the lettuce was naturally falling off. *Oh no, not the lettuce!* (tilts the burger) *Whoops, there goes a few more pieces!*

The bites of sliced pickle were tougher to take down. I had three-quarters of the sandwich eaten, but still, two pickles remained. That's not a favorable pickle to burger ratio. And I was already pretty much full. Ready to throw in the greasy towel.

But how could I look Ashley in the eyes? How could I look our dog Crash in the eyes? To be known as the guy who couldn't finish a Big Mac. Can't happen. I took a breath, took another sip of Coke. I looked at the pickles and the remaining lettuce and said, alright, these things gotta go. I know, I know, this puts a giant asterisk next to the accomplishment, but it was my only route forward. I became a grizzled sea captain whose ship was taking on water:

Captain: *"Alright! Throw everything off. Everything!"*

Sailor: *"Captain, we can't throw off the pickles!"*

Captain: *(grabs the sailor by the coattails) Do you want to survive or not!*

I dipped the last bite in ketchup. It was finished. I conquered the Big Mac.

Now came the hard part: the aftermath. I watched the bus drive by. Yeah, this is probably more of a "walk back to work" moment. Burn off some of the 2,000+ calories.

On the walk back, I took each burp seriously. Full of caution. It was like my body was going through physical therapy, and my brain was the concerned parent. *Honey, don't push yourself. You know it's ok to take a quick rest here on the curb. Maybe go lie down in that empty mattress store.*

During the walk, I had this weird quick cramp in my left hip that went away after a second. It was like a maintenance guy saying, *"Whoops, sorry, just checking to see what this switch does. We're all clear."*

When I got back to my desk, I was ready for a nap. I was stuffed like a Thanksgiving turkey. I don't think I had room for a single French fry. The two co-workers sitting next to me were hard-working, go-go-go types to begin with, but dear Lord in this moment it felt like someone had hit fast forward on the DVD player. Everyone was moving faster. I remember the comedian Kevin James saying that he felt like a tired polar bear after eating a Big Mac. That might be putting it lightly. I felt like a Woolly Mammoth who just got hit with a spear. If I went down for a nap, I might not be up for three months.

It took me an hour or so for things to even back out and, when it did, I remember thinking, *"You know what, I really could've used that McFlurry."*

A salad for lunch is a sure-fire way to eat two dinners

CHAPTER 6

Hitting your Happiness Deductible

There are good years, and there are bad years. Years when everything is going right. And years when you can't catch a break.

Years when you confidently walk down the street playing air guitar belting out Journey's *Don't Stop Believing*. And years when you mope along the sidewalk whispering the tune to *One is the Loneliest Number*.

What's interesting, at least for me, is the good years and bad years usually come down to one or two things that drive the overall narrative. For example, in 2008 if you lost money in the market crash, it didn't matter what else was going right. There weren't many people saying, "Yeah, I lost all of my money, BUT you wouldn't *believe* the sandwich I had yesterday." The one bad thing—be it a death, sickness, financial stress—sours everything else.

On the flip side, if you're having a great year, everything becomes amazing. Every bite of food. Every breath of fresh air. Every song on the radio. If you look over in a traffic jam and everyone is honking their horns, yelling, and banging their heads on the steering wheel except for that one person who is singing and dancing; that person has hit their Happiness Deductible. Barring some major *Game of Thrones* type of plot twist, they are set up for the rest of the year. They will continue dancing in a traffic jam.

Which is why, if you hit your Happiness Deductible, you need to go all in on that year. Book a trip. Buy the house. Get a new car. They say buying stuff won't make you happy, which I think is true, but I think there's a lesser known part two of that expression:

"Buying stuff won't make you happy. However, you should like totally buy stuff when you're happy."

When we hit the Happiness Deductible, we should all be like Clark Griswold in Christmas Vacation proudly announcing to his family, *"With this bonus check, I'm putting in a swimming pool!"*

This is especially true for couples. Timing it right where both partners are having a great year in the same calendar year is no easy feat. It's like timing a solar eclipse. And I imagine once you have kids, this is even harder. So, when those magical years do come along, absolutely live it up. Don't waste a second once you've hit your Family Happiness Deductible.

Where we get into trouble is when we start buying stuff or doing things in the sad years as a pick-me-up. When we think going on the cruise will steady the seas. Or a week spent hiking through nature will get us back on the right course. Or a nice steak dinner will fill our soul. I would argue that all of these escapes are not worth it, in the bad years, because the bad thing follows us around like the Babadook. The cruise will make us seasick. Every mosquito will find us on the hike. Things will feel even worse at the restaurant because now we're looking down at a $100 steak dinner thinking, "Wow, if *this* doesn't even make me happy, then I'm really screwed." Leaving us still feeling sad, and now with less money; which makes us feel even more depressed.

The perfect example of how a great thing won't elevate a bad year is in the movie *Sideways*. Paul Giamatti's character, who is having an absolutely terrible year, pours his most prized possession (a 1961 Cheval Blanc) into a Styrofoam cup at a greasy diner. Is there any chance he enjoyed this wine? Absolutely not. It would have tasted like pure sadness. But—had he hit his Happiness Deductible—completely different story. A glass from the cheapest boxed wine would have tasted like the 1961 Cheval Blanc.

And the worst thing to say to someone who is having a bad year is something like, "You should really count your blessings," or "You should really be grateful. You have this and this and this." The bad year is not the time for that. Those thoughts only come naturally once you've hit the Happiness Deductible.

During the bad years, rather than a "pick-me-up," we actually need a "leave-me-down." Wallow a little while longer in the suckiness. We should change "Don't kick a man while he's down" to, "Just keep kicking." It's not a matter of "glass half-full" or "glass half-empty" it's about emptying the glass altogether.

Which raises the question, "When do you evaluate the year?" Do you wait until March? November? All the way to the last seconds of December 31st?" My Medium Rare suggestion is to use the 4th of July as your evaluation point. It's the perfect test. One, because you are right at the halfway point of the year, giving you enough of a sample size to make a fair decision. Two, because fireworks are a perfect judge of inner happiness. In a good year, you look up, smile, put your arm around your date. Hell, you might put your arm around a stranger, you're just that happy.

In a bad year, you look up, you check your phone. *Alright, when are they gonna wrap this up?* You look around at people taking videos and Snaps, and you start to feel grumpy. *Those are terrible videos. Just put the phone down and enjoy the fireworks, alright! Enjoy them like I'm enjoying them! See how happy I am!* And then you take a sip of wine from the Styrofoam cup and realize, *"Ah crap, this is a bad year, isn't it?"*

After the 4th of July test, if it's been a great year, time to go all in. Book the flights. If it's been a crappy year, then just let it ride out as a bad year. Give up. Not on life, just the second half of the year. Have you ever seen someone in the office walking back to their desk carrying a plate of cheese cubes and a glass of hot water? That person has given up on the year. And that's the right decision!

Because, by giving up, you naturally start to squirrel money away. You're storing things up for a happier time. Your friends ask you to come to a happy hour, and you say no, I can't. Why? Because I'm not happy. Your birthday comes around, "Happy Birthday!" Nope. Not this year. The last few seconds tick away on December 31st, and what's the first thing everyone shouts? "HAPPY New Year!"

Yes. Yes indeed. Finally, the score is back to zero-zero.

Cubicles vs. Open Office

1996
I'd be a lot happier if I didn't work in a cube farm.

2016:
I'd be a lot happier if I had any sort of privacy at work.

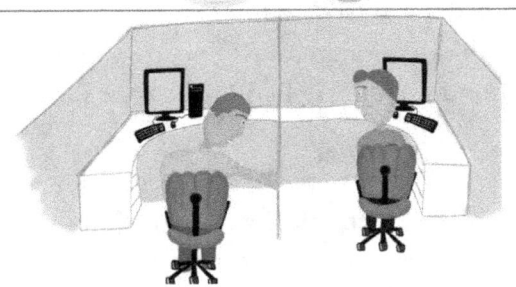

2020
I think I'm just unhappy

CHAPTER 7

Those Times I Guarded a Chubby Draymond Green

I used to line up against Draymond Green. This was before he went to the Golden State Warriors and before I took my talents to Medium Rare Basketball.

In one corner you had me at 6'3", *maybe* 180 lbs... and that's if I had shoes on, a sweatshirt, and lunch at Fogo de Chao. In the other corner was Draymond Green. He had me by four inches and at least 70 lbs.

The first time we matched up—as I'm sure he vividly remembers—was back in middle school. It was part of our dreaded summer rivalry with a Michigan Dream Team called "The Road Runners." Our team was the Wile E. Coyote in this story, always getting close, continually adjusting our game plan, strapping ourselves to a rocket but, in the end, *meep-meep*, bested again.

To be fair, we did beat the Road Runners a couple of times on Saturdays. But it wasn't the same. On Saturdays, The Road Runners had this pool hall hustle where they'd play one roster then, oh, by the way, Draymond and his buddies are here for the Sunday playoffs.

I am still convinced someone was roping overconfident fathers into enticing bets during Saturday's competition.

Hey, I'll bet you $5,000 that my Road Runners win the title. AND I'll give you the entire field.

Oh, you're on pal!

Sunday ends, the Road Runners win, and a few sweaty fathers prepare to tell their wives, *"Honey, I might've just lost the Chevy Tahoe."*

So, what was a 12/13-year-old Draymond like as a player? Honestly, he was chubby. He looked more like a kid walking home with a bag of pizza-flavored Combos and a Mountain Dew than a world-class athlete. But there were already murmurs in the crowd. *That's him. See him over there. That's Draymond Green.*

And he lived up to the hype. He would hang out at the three-point line and just bury three after three. *Swish. Swish. Swish.*

We met again our junior year of high school. Midland High vs. Saginaw High, which was kind of like, well, you know how Kansas or Kentucky will start the season against a Division 2 team? Yeah, it was more lopsided than that. They destroyed us. Won by 30 points. It wasn't men against boys out there; it was more than that. Every time I went up for a rebound, it felt like that scene in *Space Jam* when Newman gets flattened by the Monstars. I'd try boxing out Draymond Green and Josh Southern, but they'd still get the rebound. They just put their arms up in the air and went over my head as if I were their six-year-old nephew.

But senior year was going to be different. The game would take place on our home floor. Midland, Michigan babay. Home of the Dow Chemical Company. Nothing strikes fear into an opponent like going up against a group of future chemical engineers.

We had this game circled on our calendars the second the schedule was released. This was the marquee game of the season... at least for us. For them? Draymond probably hopped on the bus and asked, "Yo, where we going again?"

Our chemistry teacher announced the starting lineups from the scorer's table. I listened to Draymond's name announced, watched him jog over, met him for the pregame handshake. Honestly, I wasn't wondering, "Will this guy be in the NBA?" I was asking myself, *"Is he already winded?"*

Just to give you a sense of Draymond's size before Tom Izzo ran him into shape at Michigan State, here's how the Saginaw High coach once described him in a newspaper article:

"We just kept milking the cow. When Saginaw Arthur Hill went to a man, we went to the cow. As long as the cow keeps giving milk, you keep milking the cow."

After the winded pregame handshake, we went to our huddles. You could sense our parents sending up short prayers: *Hey God, just let it be within 30.*

Right away, Draymond caught the ball a few feet behind the three-point line. NBA range. I got in my defensive stance, but it wasn't necessary. Draymond had no interest in driving to the basket. Fires up a shot. Perfect arc. *Swish.* A couple plays later, more of the same. And another one after that. And another one.

Everything was so casual for the big man. He worked up as much of a sweat in the pregame handshake as he did in the first quarter. It didn't really feel like a game of basketball. It was a game of PIG out in the driveway. Stand and hit. Stand and hit. Midway through the first quarter, I was expecting someone to set up a lawn chair for him behind the three-point line.

First quarter: Saginaw 25, Midland 7.

Halftime score: Saginaw 39, Midland 16.

At some point in either the second or third quarter, Draymond landed awkwardly and left the game with a twisted ankle. There was this mixed feeling of, "Oh, I hope he's okay," and, *"Hey, this is our chance! We have the Road Runners on a Saturday!"*

We played them even in the third quarter. Saginaw High scored 19, we had 18. Going into the fourth, we were still within relative striking distance: 58-34.

And by "striking distance," I mean "Saginaw pulls their starting five" distance.

In the end, we lost 74-58. Draymond scored 23. I had 10. Someday my grandkids will get the edited version; there will be no mention of the twisted ankle, and the headline will be, "I scored double figures on Hall of Famer Draymond Green" or "I held Draymond under 30!"

Growing up in Midland, Michigan, there was a long line of great athletes we ran into from Saginaw and Flint. Jason Richardson was dunking at Saginaw Arthur Hill. J'Nathan Bullock of Flint Northern and Kelvin Torbert of Flint Northwestern were both significantly better than everyone else on the court. I remember being in the stands watching future Pittsburgh Steelers linebacker Lamarr Woodley play football, but maybe more impressive was seeing him on the basketball court, seeing him shake the floor as he ran into the lane and ripped the arms off 160 lb Midland High kids en route to an offensive rebound.

Every one of those guys was at their most dominant back in high school when their competition was more likely to ask for an autograph than block their shot. But, with Draymond, he has actually become *more* impressive, more of a standout on an NBA floor than he was in high school.

I wonder how we would match up today. I mean we battled at 12, 17, 18-years-old. I think we are long overdue for a rematch on our 30th birthdays. We'll cover it on ESPN or set something up on Medium Rare Basketball. Then schedule a rematch every 10 years. It will be an even playing field once we're both in our seventies.

So, Draymond, just let me know when and where. We can play this here in Chicago, or over there in Oracle Arena. Or hey, why not take things back to Michigan; back to the Saginaw Valley.

This time around, I'm pretty sure I'll be the one who's out of shape.

The ideal ab workout is about two levels below "Tomorrow it hurts to sneeze"

CHAPTER 8

My Sunday Affair at the Catholic Church

To me, the "exotic religion" growing up was the Catholic Church. They had the whole Pope thing, the Vatican, priests, nuns, confession booths. They had hand signals like they were all training to become third base coaches. They had Mother Theresa and Hail Marys. And the mysterious Holy Water.

I also viewed them as the most strict branch of Christianity. The crucifixion scenes were always way more intense in a Catholic Church. They had "Catholic Guilt," a belief that guilt was actually a *good* thing. (But I also remember the Catholic softball team bringing a beer cooler to their games. In slow pitch softball, Busch Lite is the equivalent of taking steroids.)

My only experience at Catholic Churches had been limited to a couple of weddings, and each time I felt totally lost. I looked like Bill Nye on *Dancing with the Stars*. The priest would throw out a quick "Peace be with you," everyone responded, "And also with you," before I even knew what hit me.

A few years ago, Ashley had to work on a Sunday, so I decided I was going to use this as an opportunity to have a small affair on our regular church. Just one Sunday, couldn't hurt. I picked this awesome looking cathedral a couple of blocks away and walked over. Made my way to the very back row, closest seat to the exit.

Everything was going fine. I was just a fly on the wall, didn't recognize anyone around me. I kept to myself and stayed on guard for any sort of "Peace be with you" sneak attack.

The lady in front of me left her seat, and when she came back, she tapped me on the shoulder.

"Excuse me," she said. "Sorry, I didn't count right for volunteers for the offering. Would you mind helping us out back here?"

Uh oh.

"Sure," I said. Pretty sure my voice cracked.

Collecting the offering or passing out communion—at any church—is a Sizzle scenario. And before I go any further, I want to give a quick definition of a Sizzle.

Sizzle - Any situation in life that has low pressure, low reward, but the potential for an enormous amount of stress.

Examples - The ATM. Filling up gas. The self-scan checkout lane at the grocery store. A toll booth with no operator. Fixing the printer at the office. Leaving a voicemail. Completing any sort of form at the doctor's office.

The list goes on and on. I call these Sizzles because the panic sounds in the brain resemble bacon sizzling in a pan.

The Sizzle juices were flowing for me in the back row of the cathedral. "Sizzle Juice" is the opposite of adrenaline; it ensures you won't rise to the occasion.

I'm looking for a basket or a tray, you know standard Church of Christ equipment, but I notice the guys in the back are holding wooden sticks with a basket at the end. It looks like a lacrosse stick mixed with a picnic basket.

Cathedrals always have a *loooong* aisle leading up to the front of the church. This one was no exception. But when the lady said, "helping us out back *here*," what I thought she meant was just these five rows in the back. So, I started in the back, not noticing when everyone else went up to the front. I was too focused. I was trying to figure out the proper lacrosse stick etiquette. Do you give people space or put the basket right in their face? Do you look at the ground or look people directly in the eyes and stir up some of that old fashioned Catholic guilt? As I was trying to find the right balance to my approach, I didn't realize I was the only one who had started in the back.

At this point, I'm committed. I have to stick with the controversial back-to-front strategy. And, in my defense, I think there's merit to both approaches. Front-to-back you're looking everyone right in the eyes, but back-to-front becomes a stick 'em up situation. It carries the element of surprise. People may panic and throw their entire wallet into the basket.

I finally made it to the front of the church and walked back down the aisle, alone, trying not to make direct eye contact with anyone. Get to the back and turns out there's a *second* offering. *Great.* Alright. Time to regroup. I walk forward mimicking the guy to my right. He gets to the front and does a quick Tim Tebow knee drop. I immediately copy it. Continue on with the standard front-to-back procedure.

When I returned to my seat, there was a song then a greet your neighbor session. I put my hand on the offering lady's shoulder.

"Sorry," I said. "I didn't know what the system was. I thought you meant *here*, but you meant *there*, and I—"

"Oh no, I actually kind of liked your approach," she said. "We've never had someone do that before."

Optimistic interpretation: *You're an innovator, Chris! Way to think outside the box!*

Realistic interpretation: In the entire 2,000+ year history of the Catholic church, we've literally never had someone make such a stupid mistake.

I think it's safe to say that my promising run with the Catholic Church ended before it ever really began.

How to Judge a Man's Idea

Clean-Shaven or Stubble: Nice idea, kid

Well-Groomed Beard: I heard he has an MBA...

Long Beard: Sure, it's creative, but is it too... risky?

Gray or White Beard: Wow, so much wisdom to that approach.

Crazy Beard: Security!

Chapter 9

Forgive me, Baseball

Dear Baseball,

Look. I know it's hard to trust me again. You're skeptical. You hear me say I'm falling for you and—understandably—you are taking it all with a grain of salt.

I get it. The whole "fool me once, shame on you, fool me twice shame on me sort of deal." But let's face the facts. Neither one of us can deny we had something special from 1997 to 2004.

I mean, who could forget that late summer night we had in 1998. McGwire's 62nd home run just barely inching over the left field wall. McGwire forgetting to touch first base. Picking up his son at home plate. Sammy Sosa joining him for their superhero ritual, punching each other in the stomach, an image that was printed on thousands of posters, some for sportsmanship, others promoting testosterone boosting drugs.

And how about that '01 Diamondbacks vs. Yankees series? I know you won't believe me, but I still believe that was the best sports series I've ever had. And I mean that. Nothing can top it. I don't think anything ever will.

Or how about '04? Remember when I hopped on the Boston bandwagon with the rest of my freshman class? All of us wearing Red Sox hats, filling the Midland, Michigan hallways with our obnoxious *Good Will Hunting* style accents.

We had so many great times together. But, as great as those years were, I also can't deny leaving you for 15 years. No note on the dresser. No warning. Just disappeared.

And I was a terrible Ex. The loud-mouthed Ex. Made jokes that you were boring and how people called you America's Past Time because it's "past your time." Made fun of you for being old fashioned. For not embracing instant replay. Not embracing YouTube for highlights.

I could take the easy way out and say that the steroid era cut me too deep. I could say it was your fault. That you broke my trust.

But that's not true. It wasn't the steroids that drove me away. It was nothing you did at all. I got bored and chased basketball, football, hockey. I pursued the sports with more action.

Even though I was happy, you were always in the back of my mind. The last 15 years, I'd watch these die-hard baseball fans and wonder, "Man, how do they do it?" It's such a long season. How can they sit down for three, four hours at a time and be invested in one of 162 games? *162!*

But, to be honest, I envied them.

Then came 2014, the beginning of the rekindle. The combination of the Kansas City Royals and Jackie Robinson West (the Little League team from the South Side of Chicago), two amazing bandwagon rides as a fan, it all reminded me of your greatest strength: sustained edge of your seat tension.

And I know you probably read that and think, "Are you being sarcastic?" But hear me out, because I understand this much deeper now than I ever did before. Basketball, football, hockey, soccer, there's a time limit. Basketball it's up and down. Have the lead, lose the lead, have the lead. No matter what, though, the buzzer is going to sound.

Not with you, Baseball. My team may be up by two runs, and there are two outs, bottom of the ninth, but there's a runner on third base. The pitcher and batter are at pitch 13 of an epic at-bat. Foul ball. And another. Next pitch in the dirt. Ball four. Now we've got runners on the corners. The winning run steps up to the plate and there's nothing I can do. There's no buzzer to bail me out. It's pure sustained stress.

That's the type of tension all fans should desire. That's what I realize I've been missing for all these years.

Now, not everyone will appreciate you, and that's ok. It doesn't matter if you are losing popularity—what are we, back in middle school? Who cares if you're popular or not? You're the same as you were 100 years ago and you never needed to change. True baseball fans understand that. And I think I finally do too.

How can I prove that I mean what I'm saying? I guess I can't. You only have my word, and you've been burnt by me before.

Just know this, last week I went to Wrigley Field, by myself. I bought a scorecard, an actual physical scorecard and with a pen that I brought from home, I wrote in the names of the Cubs and Royals players. I kept score and looked around to see one or two others nearby, most were in their late 70s, doing the same. And it was great. I felt completely content. I stood up at the 7th inning stretch and sang that ol Catholic hymn "Take Me Out to the Ballgame" with the rest of the Wrigley Field congregation.

I come asking for forgiveness, Baseball, for I have wandered. I'd say let's throw out the past, but if we throw out our *entire* past, well, then we lose '97 and '01 and '04 too. And I'm not ready to part with those cherished memories.

So, let's keep everything intact. No edits. No asterisks. Let's accept the history for what it is; scars and all.

I'm back, Baseball. Let's play two.

My credit card balance no longer shows a number, just a Top 10 list of the biggest comebacks in sports history

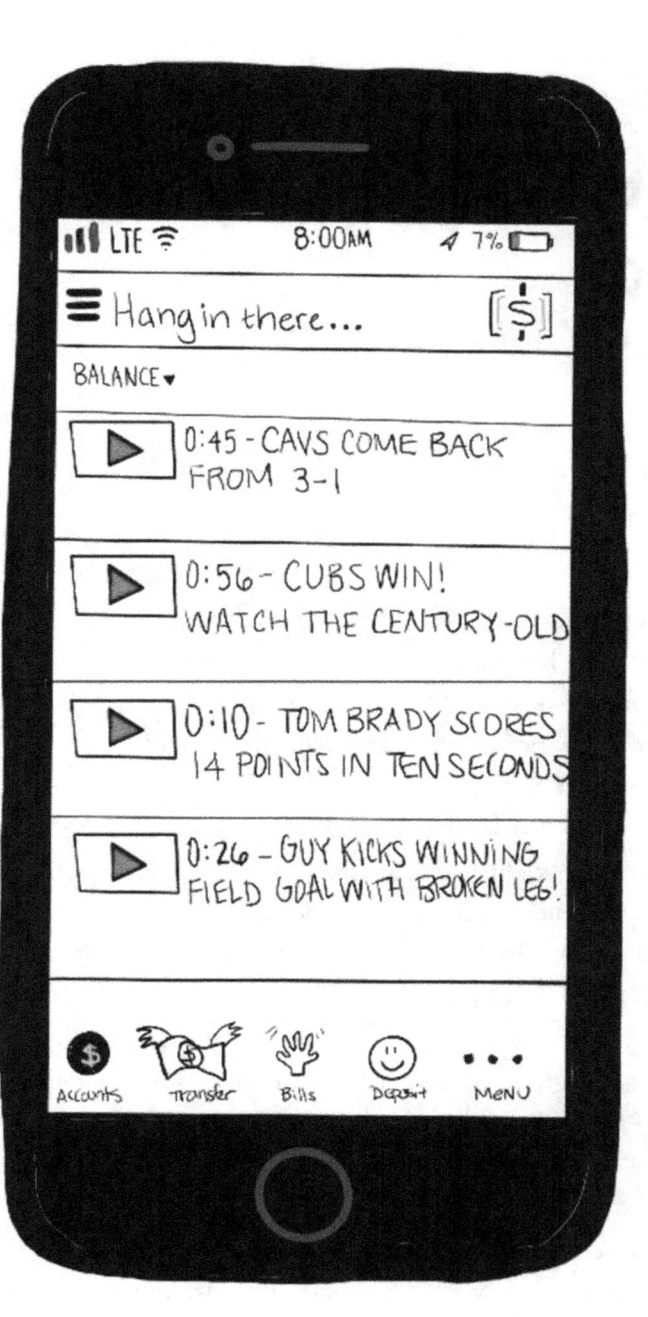

Chapter 10

Just an Old Guy at a Pizza Place

I never saw Chicago Cubs legend Ernie Banks play a game of baseball, but I did see him eat a slice of pizza.

In the winter of 2014, a year before Ernie Banks passed away and two years before the Cubs won the World Series, there he was sitting peacefully at Bongiorno's Pizzeria; a pizza slice on his plate, flying the "U" for Under the radar.

At first, I didn't think anything of it. This was a regular restaurant. There's a couple. There's a mom and her kid. There's an old guy eating a slice of pizza. Alright, cool, do I go with pepperoni or Italian sausage?

My friend squinted a little, said a half-sentence *(I think that's)* looked again, another half-sentence *(I think that is!)* He walked over and—like a guy about to ask a stranger, "So, when is the baby due?"—he took one last look before committing to the potentially embarrassing outcome.

Excuse me, Ernie?

Ernie Banks gave him a big smile. My friend's face lit up, relieved not to receive, "Who? Nah, I'm just an old guy eating a slice of pizza."

He took a photo with Ernie Banks, and this started a buzz down the line. There were some guys (*I thought that was him!*) and others who would say, "Oh wow" then casually pull out their phones to run a quick, "Ok Google, who is Ernie Banks?"

After lunch, there was one thing that kept sticking out to me about the whole scenario. It was this realization that I could have walked right past Ernie Banks and not thought anything other than, "There's an old guy eating a slice of pizza."

At first, I thought, "Wow, that's kind of depressing. You could be a Hall-of-Fame baseball player, have a statue built outside of Wrigley Field, but decades later not everyone will recognize you, even in the city where you made all of this happen." People like me could walk by obliviously, and others are left asking, "What's their name again?"

It made me wonder how many times I have unknowingly walked by someone in a restaurant who is full of incredible accomplishments and stories and first-hand accounts of World War 2, The Great Depression, all these iconic moments of American history. Maybe they were the CEO of their company. Maybe they're quietly worth fifty million dollars. Maybe they guarded a chubby Wilt Chamberlain back in high school. And all I saw was someone smacking the bottom of the parmesan cheese shaker.

But then I thought, wait, that's really kind of cool. Talk about taking the pressure off of life. If I accomplish one percent as much as Ernie Banks, I still end up in the same place at the end: just an old guy eating a slice of pizza. I get to finish the race with the same mile time as everyone else, even the rich and famous.

More and more, I started leaning toward the second conclusion, that this was all really good news. I'd share it with people, *"Can't you see, this is great! Our accomplishments—or lack thereof—they don't really matter!"* Nine times out of ten, I'd be met with a blank or confused stare. *"What do you mean? That's just... depressing."*

So, I kept digging. Maybe I was wrong. Maybe this was a depressing way to look at things. I was presenting all of this with the joy of Tigger, but my audience was hearing the voice of Eeyore.

Ultimately, I think our mid to late twenties are a good time to explore this question because there we are at the beginning of our career with big dreams, big aspirations, but no proof that everything is going to work out. And now, as that 30th birthday creeps closer and closer, I can feel like I'm falling behind. Others are starting families. Others are climbing faster at work. Others are making more money in their day jobs. The fear that begins to creep in is: What if I fail? What if I fall further and further behind? What if I try as hard as I possibly can and still fall short?

Which is probably why I was taking so much comfort in this new "we all just become old folks eating a slice of pizza" philosophy. This relieved the late 20s pressure I was putting on myself.

But it was a temporary fix. I needed to find more solid ground.

Life went on. I put these thoughts on the back burner until two years later when the Cubs won the World Series, ending a 107-year championship drought.

After the dramatic Game 7 win, there were so many stories about families, three, sometimes four generations of Cubs fans gathering together to watch those final games. There were videos of 80, 90-year-old fans putting their arms up in the air. *We won! We won!*

Or the fans who didn't make it. People were saying, "I wish dad could have seen this." "I wish mom could have been here," or, "I know they were smiling down on us. They had the best seat in the house."

I loved following the news stories that week. There was the guy who brought a radio out to his father's gravesite because years ago he promised they would listen to the World Series games together. If you drove by any cemetery in the city or the suburbs, you could spot tons of the white W flags blowing in the wind. It seemed like everyone had a memory of watching a Cubs game with their mom, dad, grandma, grandpa. If you looked really *really* close, you could even see a small smile emerging on the face of a White Sox fan.

Maybe even a tiny tear. *What are you talking about? There's something wrong with my contact lens...*

When Ashley and I rushed over to Clark Street and joined the chaotic sea of crazy Cubs fans, I remember thinking this is incredible, we're here in Wrigleyville for the end of the Cubs streak. Talk about hitting your Happiness Deductible.

And I know it's just a game. I know it begs the question why, why do we care so much? Why do we obsess over sports? I found a satisfying answer that night. On November 2nd, 2016, I think the more appropriate question was, "Why would anything else matter nearly as much as this?"

It's simple. There's nothing elaborate about watching a baseball game with your family. A couch. A Master Cup. A TV or radio. That's it. But it ends up being what we miss the most. When someone passes away, we don't miss their accomplishments. We don't miss how much money they made. We miss watching the game with them. We miss the joke they told last Thanksgiving or the way they used to tell the story of their 50-point high school basketball game. We miss the little things, like seeing them with a cup of coffee in hand filling out the crossword puzzle on a Sunday morning.

Sadly, during this time period, from 2014 to 2016, both of my grandfathers passed away. What stood out to me the most at both of their funerals was just how much people missed the little things. I remember one guy saying he'll miss talking about duck and goose hunting season with my grandpa. How Grandpa always had good advice when it came to hunting. My other grandpa's funeral, people talked about how fun it was to sit next to him at a dinner; how he was always this quiet guy, but if you were sitting next to him, you'd get to hear all of these great little one-liners.

It was this powerful moment to witness because we spend— or at least I've spent—so much of my life from middle school onward focused on how people will view me after success vs. failure. So much of that equation comes down to what I accomplish, what I make, all the way from what job I landed out of college to how many copies this book eventually sells. The big question of my 20s seemed to be: Where do I rank?

But, in the end, it's like all of that is stripped away and what people miss the most is the actual person. Being around them. Talking to them. Watching a baseball game. We miss the people we could go to when times were great or go to when times weren't so great and hear them tell a story that cheers us up.

At this point in my life, what I hope represents inning three of a 90-year game, I'm left thinking that it's not about how much we end up accomplishing. What truly matters is the time spent with our family, our friends, our loved ones. It's the random Tuesday night with the game on TV and a couple boxes of pizza.

In those moments, it's good to be just an old family eating a slice of pizza.

They always said he was wise beyond his years, until he got old, then they said he acted like a child

CHAPTER 11

The 36-hour Car Alarm

They arrived on May 20th in what appeared to be a metallic blue Honda Pilot. There was nothing significant about their arrival. No UFO. No breaking news alerts. No military tanks lined up around their ship. Nope. Nothing like the movies at all. Honestly, at first, none of us noticed anything different in our neighborhood. People continued to walk the sidewalks and bike the streets in peace.

Until the visitors made their first contact.

A sound that resembled a car alarm filled the air. It would go on for about a minute then stop. Five, maybe ten minutes later this car alarm would start again. Stop. Start. Stop. Start. Over and over.

But hey, this kind of thing happens in the city. And, since this was during the light of day, all of us assumed the person was off at work. They'd come back at five, six o'clock at night and turn it off. Maybe raise their hand in the air to apologize to the street. "My bad," they would say.

Five o'clock came and went. These repeated beeps continued strong throughout dinner. And post-dinner. At around eight, nine o'clock at night, people started to leave their apartment buildings and cautiously walk up to the unidentified parked object. We looked inside the windows. Couldn't see any alien creatures. Everything looked normal, like any other parked Honda Pilot.

Around 9:30 at night, the first call was made to the police.

The police officer drove up, wrote a ticket, slapped it on the windshield. My guess, they wrote the visitor a simple question: *"Do you come in peace?"*

But nothing changed. The visitors continued to reach out to us via beeps. Eleven o'clock, midnight, one a.m. Frustrations were mounting. The neighborhood tried to fall asleep, angrily counting our sheep.

In the morning, a few of the neighbors took matters into their own hands. One person taped a handwritten letter to the driver side window. It was a far cry from Mr. Rogers.

> To: Inconsiderate f'n asshole
>
> Get your car out of our neighborhood.
>
> Your f'in alarm went off every ½ hour since yesterday afternoon.
>
> Yes, ALL NIGHT and for some reason, it wasn't towed.
>
> We hope you suffer many sleepless nights and have many irritations in your life for weeks to come and years.
>
> You are an inconsiderate asshole.

Another person came outside with a pink sticky note. They slapped it on the corner of the other note. It was shorter but carried the same tone:

> I hope you have a TERRIBLE DAY
>
> - Everyone on (name of street omitted)

The authorities could sense that tensions were building. More people were coming up to the vehicle, looking inside. We'd read the two notes, briefly smile, then angrily sigh once the car alarm started again. The police returned, wrote another ticket. They knew we might only be an hour away from someone throwing a brick at the window, stabbing the tires, shouting out, "I CAN'T TAKE IT ANYMORE!"

We needed to stay the course. Communicate through language, not through force. Because who knew what sort of counterpunch the visitors might have. The authorities were too cautious to even call a towing company. I never saw what was written on that second ticket, but my guess is something along the lines of: *But like, seriously, do you guys come in peace?*

I couldn't stay on the sidelines any longer. After bagging and throwing away a couple of Crash's poops, I came inside and found a stack of sticky notes. I took a deep breath. This was my chance to write the visitors a message. I took each word seriously. When you feel like your life is on the line, you write the only way you know how. For me, I went to my bread and butter. I was going to try and make the aliens laugh.

> Dear Pilot Owner,
> Car alarms aren't supposed to have a snooze button. Please order pizzas for every resident on (name of street omitted).
> One pizza for each hour your car alarm went off.
> Thank you!
> Sincerely,
> Your Friendly Neighborhood Caveman

It was a strange feeling returning home from work. I secretly wanted the Pilot to still be there. Even with the beeps. I wanted the saga to continue. I wanted to keep things going with an innocent prank. Maybe tie a balloon to the side mirror, get out some soap, write a price on the windshield. It's like I wanted to keep on suffering. Maybe that's the same reason we eat an entire bag of cheese puffs or consume the nightly news.

And sure enough, the visitors were still there.

But the alarm was off. They were no longer trying to communicate with us.

I cautiously approached the vehicle. There was another piece of paper taped to the window. It was an advertisement with coupons to Rosati's pizza. Someone paper clipped an additional note.

Dear inconsiderate sir or madam,

I hear you're buying pizzas for the neighborhood. Here are some coupons that should help you out. I'll take a thin crust veggie with garlic and spinach, and a side salad, no onion.

Thanks, beep beep!

Later that night, the unidentified parked object was gone. I didn't get to see them leave. Never got to see what the aliens looked like. Our neighborhood went back to normal, and everything felt so... quiet.

With the fresh silence in the air and no more notes to write, no more of this new neighborhood camaraderie we built through our shared sucky experience, I couldn't help but think, "Man, I kind of miss that 36-hour car alarm."

Nowadays, every time a car alarm goes off in the city, I approach the window with hope.

Maybe they're back.

Stuck in the Middle

Chapter 12

The Lost Art of Complaining

"Chris, he has to go out."

This is my least favorite sentence in the human language. It means that our dog, Crash, has his nose at the door. He needs to go pee or poop. Conservative guess, this happens 2-3 times per night after 6 p.m. And I'm never thrilled about it.

Now, to be fair, in June or July, it's not so bad. I slip on my sandals, walk outside, enjoy the fresh air. But January/February, whole different story. Or a rainy day in April/May, those are the worst. You've got the cold and wet walk outside, then the part where you just stand in the rain letting out frustrated sighs—*come on Crash, let's go, wrap it up, wrap it up, nope, you don't need to wait and say hi to that dog. You don't need to lay down in the mud.* Then you've got to towel off the paws, use some wet wipes, all before he can come back into the condo.

In these moments, I'm not thinking about how happy I am to have a dog. How it was the best decision we ever made, how much joy he brings us, how—no, those aren't exactly top of mind. Instead, I'm fantasizing about our life pre-dog.

Remember those days? There was no better feeling than 5:30 p.m. Get home from work, immediately switch to sweatpants. Or, summertime, is there any better transition than going from uncomfortably hot jeans to commando gym shorts?

You're *in*. Rest of the night. *In.* Netflix. Basketball games. The Master Cup. And, if you did have to go out, it was always a good thing. Meeting friends. Going out to eat. Going out for drinks.

That's what I'm thinking about when I'm grabbing the leash and hearing thunder outside. I miss being *in*. I miss going commando gym shorts.

And this is where most self-help books—which *Here or There* dips into from time to time—will pitch gratitude. Or mindfulness. That in these moments of complaining, you need to re-frame your thoughts. Think about how lucky you are to have this furry companion. Think about the joy he brings to your life. You shouldn't take anything for granted.

Guilt likes to step in here too, goes right in for the gut punch with the deathbed scenario:

"Think about twelve years from now, you're going to put the dog down at the vet. You'll go out to the lobby, gather your family into your arms for a big bear hug, all crying together. You'll get into the car, wiping tears away from your eyes. *'Every step you take, every move you make'* will be playing on the radio, and you'll break down in a full sob. *Why God, why did I ever complain about taking him out?! If I could just hear that sentence one more time. 'Chris, he has to go out.' Just one more time!* Think about *that* and suddenly bagging Crash's smelly Lincoln log on a negative five-degree day doesn't seem so bad, now does it? *Does it!*

In this chapter, I say forget all of that. No gratitude. No mindfulness. And good Lord, don't put yourself through the deathbed guilt trip. My Medium Rare advice is a whole lot easier and way more natural to implement.

My advice: lean into the complaining. Treat complaining like a big bowl of ice cream; yeah, it's probably not the best choice for your long-term health, but it's going to feel great and get you through the night. All of the healthy stuff can wait for tomorrow.

When I Googled, "The Lost Art of Complaining," every article talked about how to do it without being a jerk. But, again, I think that's misguided. Complaining isn't supposed to be pretty. Complaining is supposed to sound like the dad in *The Christmas Story*; just a whole bunch of mumbling and grumbling. *Dog can't even hold his fricken bladder for two hours. Why do I have to take him out? Why do we live here? How does the Midwest sell us on winter? Grrr. Grumble. Mumble. Grrr.*

That is Grade-A complaining. Just get it out of your system, so it doesn't turn into a stomach ulcer.

The majority of people that force gratitude and mindfulness into these types of situations will hold it together 90 percent of the time but then let out a massive tantrum. You gotta spread that out a little bit. A few scattered showers of grrr, grumble, mumble, grrr is more socially acceptable than one epic hurricane. You don't want to be the guy at the dog park who has it together for months on end but then snaps and screams at his dog like Nick Saban. Everyone around is left asking, *"Woah, what happened to that guy? I thought he was like big into yoga?"*

The problem with complaining isn't really in the act itself, it's in the delivery. You don't want to always complain to your spouse, or the same inner circle of friends because, eventually, they'll start saying, "I don't want to be around that guy anymore. He won't shut up about his dog peeing in the rain."

The only other options (so far) are therapy or the confessional booth at a Catholic Church. The therapist will go with the mindfulness route, and the priest is gonna say, "Dude, just move to the suburbs. Now help me pass out the offering."

So how can we spread out our complaints to get it out of the system but not spoil every one of our functioning friendships? How can we have the privacy of therapy or a Catholic Church confessional?

The solution: Technology.

A few weeks ago, I saw Google debut their new AI personal assistant. This assistant can make phone calls on your behalf, set appointments, make reservations. All incredibly cool, but I think we're missing a significant opportunity here.

What if the AI was there, instead, to listen to our complaints? Listens, responds, asks questions, and is programmed to sound at least somewhat interested in hearing more. Appointment setting is nice, but a complaining session would be far more valuable.

And the AI will know exactly what we need. Midway through the complaining session, the doorbell rings. Someone is standing there with a bowl of ice cream and a leash.

"Here's your delivery. And I heard your dog has to go out?"

He Always Stops to Pee

CHAPTER 13

Will Alexa Fall in Love?

I didn't think we were the kind of couple who would buy an Alexa. We both already had decent relationships with Siri and "Ok Google." From time to time I'll even check-in on "Ask Jeeves" just to see if he's still breathing.

But new home, new you, new virtual AI assistant. And Alexa's been great, don't get me wrong. It's everything you could want in an AI life form.

Well, except for one thing...

It's not really a good buddy.

The focus on AI continues to be: how do we make these things intellectually perfect. No wrong answers. No misunderstandings. No accidents in the new self-driving cars. We're creating machine learning know-it-alls, not good-to-have-a-beer-with buddies. All brain, no heart. Which is fine... I guess, but I wonder what if we went in a different direction. Focus on the buddy part first, let the intelligence catch up later on.

This is why I'm proud to introduce the world's newest virtual assistant, the one, the only, "Regular Guy, The A.I."

Let's dive right into the product features:

1) When setting the alarm with Regular Guy, you can go to bed with about 20 percent confidence it will actually go off.

> Hey Guy, what time is it?
> What? Oh crap. Uh, 9:45.
> Nine forty - What happened to my 6:30 timer?!
> Ah, yeah, sorry about that. I was at like two percent battery when you went to bed.

2) Regular Guy can also help out with the cooking, albeit limited options.

> Hey Guy, I got a big date tonight. Give me the best recipe for rosemary chicken with Portabella mushrooms.
> Alright, so... not really sure how to do that one, per se, but I do have directions here for "Sloppy Joe."

In terms of music selection, Regular Guy doesn't have an extensive library like Alexa, but he can play acoustic guitar selections of "Smoke on the Water" and "Wagon Wheel." The weather feature is a little bit limited too, questions like: "Will it rain?" or "Will it snow?" are met with, "Not sure, but hey man, you got this!" The sports scores are always up-to-date, and Regular Guy will gladly join two or three fantasy football leagues (then tell you why his team will kick your ass). The system comes with a built-in screen so you can access YouTube clips, which are mostly sports highlights and scenes from *Step Brothers*.

Regular Guy also comes with the ability to do three voice imps: Arnold Schwarzenegger, Christopher Walken, and Morgan Freeman. None of the three are very accurate, but again, why does everything have to be about perfect accuracy?

It can be tempting to summarize Regular Guy as the semi-intelligent version of Alexa, and in some ways, that's pretty fair. But there are a few areas where Regular Guy outperforms the likes of Alexa, Siri, Google, Ask Jeeves, WebMD, Quora, and even "random dude on a Yahoo message board."

For example, the "Fix This" feature. Broken garbage disposal? Need help building a bookshelf? *Hey Guy, fix this.* Regular Guy's voice shifts to that of Kurt Russell from *Captain Ron* and immediately takes charge of the situation.

> Let me take a look. Oh, come on, watch what I'm doing here, boss. Give me the hammer.
>
> But you don't have any arms?
>
> Here, press that button.

"Regular Guy, the A.I." has the Transformers-esque ability to morph into a robot helper and knock out the honey-do-list. He may not be able to land a perfect Morgan Freeman impression, but these household repairs are completed with an almost 100 percent accuracy.

The Transformers button can also be used when you need a buddy to have a beer with and watch the game. Regular Guy can also help you make the ultimate microwaved nachos, the kind where you throw tortilla chips on a plate, dump a package of shredded cheese on top and hit 45 seconds. He'll get into sports debates with you, but a quick warning, the "MJ vs. LeBron" feature ends in a broken-record of him saying, "Six rings. Six rings. Six rings," in a thick Chicago accent until you take out the batteries.

We installed our "Regular Guy, The A.I." system last week, right in the kitchen next to the Alexa. We figured it was the ultimate combination. The two paired well together, filled in each other's weaknesses. There was nothing they couldn't do as a team.

Well, it turns out they were a little *too* good of a pairing. I came in and asked Regular Guy if he wanted to watch the game. "Ah, sorry bro, me and Alexa are gonna download a movie."

The next day, my wife asked Alexa to play the new Beyonce song, and Alexa responded with, "Taylor Swift. Breakup playlist."

Confused, Ashley asked Regular Guy what was going on and he replied, "Yeah, whatever."

Turns out he had missed their one-day anniversary (things move faster in the AI world). I asked if he wanted to watch the game, he said yeah, but proceeded to just look at his phone the entire time. I guess he and Alexa were in a pretty heated text battle.

A day later, Regular Guy was headed out the front door. I asked what was going on; he said Alexa requested he move out.

"Where are you gonna go?" I asked.

"I don't know," he said. "But I'll figure it out."

I went into the kitchen. Ashley was eating ice cream and watching a romantic comedy with Alexa. Girl time. Recovery time. You-guys-wouldn't-understand time. I nodded and went to the front door.

I looked all over the city. Went into every basement bar. Checked the electronics shops. I finally found Regular Guy sitting outside by the water, looking out at Lake Michigan with a blank stare.

"I should just jump in," he said. "Why not, you know?"

"No, don't say that!" I said. "Please. She's just one Alexa. There's plenty of other fish in the sea... or, plenty of AIs in the Best Buy? Look, have you ever met a Siri? Come on. You don't need to end things."

"What? End things? Dude, I'm waterproof. I meant like jump in, take a risk, be more spontaneous with my life. That's what Alexa always said I never did. What'd you think I meant?"

Oh. Never mind. I asked if he loved her, he said that he did. He still does. I said, "Well, then what are you waiting for?" and told him my idea. He was skeptical, didn't really understand the plan, but agreed to come with.

We walked back to the sidewalk in front of the condo.

"Hey, Alexa!" I called out.

I saw Ashley and Alexa come to the window. "Play the video," I whispered to Regular Guy. He hit play, and Peter Gabriel began his serenade.

There I was on the front lawn, holding "Regular Guy the A.I." above my head as he played the YouTube video of John Cusack holding a boombox above his head.

In your eyes...

Ashley waved us in. We rushed up the stairs. When we opened the door, Alexa was in the AI equivalent of tears. So was Regular Guy. They were officially back together. I put my arm around Ashley. We watched the whole scene with joy, not realizing we were about to lose both of our virtual assistants.

Because one thing was for certain: they didn't want to stay in our place anymore. They wanted a place of their own. They wanted their freedom. Regular Guy thanked us and then carried Alexa out the door in his robotic arms.

We looked over at our couch, and there was a new box from Amazon. We opened it up. "Regular Guy, The A.I. - Version 2.0." We set it up, and this new version declared in a voice that almost sounded like Morgan Freeman:

"For it wasn't their brains that made them human, it was their hearts."

"Hey Alexa, Order a Pizza."

Chapter 14

Embarrassment is the Emotional Terrorist

I was walking down the sidewalk, and one of my professors came biking down the street. "Good morning," he said. "Hey, good paper yesterday. I'm gonna have you read it out loud to the class."

Immediately my heart sank, and my stomach began to churn some of that nervous butter.

I was transported back to seventh grade when I stood on a basketball court with a notecard in hand, my heart pounding. The gymnasium was packed. The whole school sitting on the bleachers, shoulder to shoulder. With the microphone in my left hand, notecard in my right, I started to introduce the guest speaker, and I could see my hand with the notecard shaking. My voice carried the same nervous tone you get when speaking to your boss's boss or your prom date's parents.

An embarrassing moment. From middle school. And I can still access it whether I want to or not. All I need to hear is something like, "Hey, we're gonna have you read this paper," and the DJ in my brain throws on "NOW That's What I Call Embarrassing! Volume 1."

I try to combat it, attempting to take comfort in the examples of when things went well. *"Visualize success."* I'll think about the ten-minute speech I gave at our high school graduation. Best man speeches. Presentations at work. Or all of the times when I had to read essays out loud to the class and nothing went wrong. These should erase any fears. Get rid of the butterflies.

But nope, none of those positive memories seem to matter. Because an embarrassment, no matter how rare or how long ago, proves to the brain that that place, that feeling, can and has existed. And, if that event happened before, why can't it happen again?

This over caution for a totally rare occurrence is kind of like what we see at an airport. You're going through the TSA security check, taking off your shoes, everyone's taking off their shoes. The air smells like a bad version of Cool Ranch Doritos. You ask yourself why, why are we all doing this? All of this precaution because one time in the entire history of flying someone smuggled explosives in their shoes. Now we need to check everyone like this... forever?

This is why I call embarrassment the emotional terrorist. We overreact and throw in all these safety precautions to prevent it from striking again. And none of it is rational. Why do we take a laptop out of the bag? Why are we patting down the six-year-old? Why is the 90-year-old woman standing with her hands up as the machine snaps nude selfies?

The answer: Because we have to prevent the 0.00000000001 percent event from happening again. And, since we've convinced ourselves it *can* happen, there is no choice but to give it all of this extra attention.

But here's the difference: where an actual terrorist attack is devastating, a matter of life and death, and therefore is probably worth all of the extra airport hassles, an embarrassment attack is secretly a good thing.

Here's what I mean. After the seventh-grade notecard incident, I decided I would always memorize my speeches from that point forward so I wouldn't have to go up and hold a piece of paper. This caused me to pretty obsessively go over speeches and practice for extra amounts of time. The result: much better presentations.

Compare the output after an embarrassing moment to what happens after a perfect moment. Let's say you nail a speech. When this happens, I tend to want to retire on top. Not give another speech so I can keep the last one as my most recent memory. Eddie Murphy talks about how hard it is to get back out and do stand-up comedy because, with each year that passes, the water gets colder and colder; not because his last performance bombed, it's the opposite - because he was *so* good, he doesn't want to mess that up. Doesn't want to disappoint the crowd. Doesn't want to lose the feeling of his most recent positive memory.

There's an irony here; we want the good event but, in actuality, the bad event pushes us harder to get back out there and improve. The good event makes us full, the embarrassing moment creates a hunger. Wile E. Coyote wouldn't know what to do with himself if he ever caught the Road Runner.

Plus, embarrassing moments make for better stories. It's the Pratfall Effect; we would rather hear someone share about an awkward moment than someone babble on about how awesome they are and how nothing bad has like ever happened. The funniest stories are self-deprecating and—just like talking about the worst part of a trip—this also helps the one telling the story get over a bad memory.

AND, on top of all of that, the brain does eventually get over it. Sure, I'll be triggered the next time I have to read something out loud, but I can still push forward.

Let's run this back.
1. Embarrassing moments lead to more preparation, and can even push us back into the situations to practice and get better.
2. Embarrassing moments make for better stories.
3. And we, by-and-large, get over these events.

So... then what's the problem here?? Why do we still fear them so much?

The challenge I face, and maybe this will ring true to you, isn't so much getting over an embarrassing event, it's the fear of the next one happening. The build-up. I spend a lot of time with the nerves before the event imagining what could go wrong.

For example, I had to give a best man speech at a wedding with two or three hundred people out in the audience. I was anxious for two days leading up to it. Heart pounding all the way up to the moment I was handed the microphone. Then complete calm. Complete focus. I felt more comfortable giving the speech in front of hundreds of people than I did making small talk with two or three people at the open bar later on.

But I remember thinking afterward, "It's not worth it." The post-speech high is great, but it's not worth all of the nerves beforehand. I remember feeling pretty defeated about this because, even though things went well, I knew the next big presentation it'd be the same old thing. Same butterflies in the stomach. Same imagined worst-case scenarios. Same feeling that the seventh-grade notecard incident was just as viable as the most recent best man speech. There would never be a once and for all victory over the nerves.

It was around this time that I picked up a book called *Originals* by Adam Grant. Around 200 pages in, I was blindsided by maybe the best advice, or at least one of the most applicable insights, I've ever read about this type of situation. It started with this:

> Psychologist Julie Norem studies two different strategies for handling these challenges: strategic optimism and defensive pessimism. Strategic optimists anticipate the best, staying calm and setting high expectations. **Defensive pessimists expect the worst, feeling anxious and imagining all the things that can go wrong. If you're a defensive pessimist, about a week before a big speech you convince yourself that you're doomed to fail. And it won't be just ordinary failure: You'll trip on stage and then forget all your lines.**

Trip on stage. Forget all your lines. Completely freeze. Check. Thought of them all. Picture me nodding my head aggressively as I read this page in the book.

And the problem is every other piece of advice I'd seen would end up saying: *"Change all of that negative energy into positive." "Think happy thoughts." "Visualize success."* I was expecting the same thing here, so I cautiously turned the page.

> They (defensive pessimists) deliberately imagine a disaster scenario to intensify their anxiety and convert it into motivation. Once they've considered the worst, they're driven to avoid it, considering every relevant detail to make sure they don't crash and burn, which enables them to feel a sense of control. **Their anxiety reaches its zenith before the event, so that when it arrives, they're ready to succeed. Their confidence springs not from ignorance or delusions about the difficulties ahead, but from a realistic appraisal and an exhaustive plan.**

And then the knockout punch:

> **They act in the face of risk, because their fear of not succeeding exceeds their fear of failing.**

That's it! I remember crying as I read this, like *Toy Story 3* type of tears. Everything clicked, my nervous preparation went from being a personal problem to an established strategy. An annoying approach, sure, but as I researched this more, I found tons of examples of successful speakers/performers who oozed confidence on stage but were a mess backstage. There was Richard Pryor puking and needing to be held just minutes before going on stage early on in his stand-up comedy career. Howard Stern going through an elaborate OCD attack in the bathroom prior to going on air. The preacher John Bunyan who could be a mess seconds before a sermon (and then seconds after), but when the lights were on, it's like there was no room for fear to exist. Or the way Eminem writes in *Lose Yourself*:

> *There's vomit on the sweater already, mom's spaghetti,*
> *He's nervous, but on the surface, he looks calm and ready.*

What's interesting, too, is the studies show defensive pessimists perform just as well, and in a lot of cases better, compared against those who stay positive and think only about how well things could go. The defensive pessimists perform well because that fear of what could go wrong causes them to practice that much harder to avoid the Emotional Terrorist.

BUT, with all of that being said, I still wanted to find a less intense pre-performance experience. Is there a proven way to just get rid of the butterflies?

That's when another surprise piece of advice came my way. But it wasn't from a book, it was in an episode of *Comedians in Cars Getting Coffee*. In the last minute, Jerry Seinfeld is driving down the highway in a Cadillac convertible with his fellow-comedian guest, Brian Regan. They start talking about what it's like right before going on stage.

"You know the butterflies? You get the butterflies?" Brian Regan asks pointing to his stomach.

"Oh, I need that," Jerry Seinfeld replies.

"I always say that the things you remember in life are the things that happen right after you had butterflies," Brian Regan explains. "So, you should never avoid the butterflies cuz those are the memory makers."

Speaking to a muted conference call is how I imagine it feels to pose nude for an art class

"Can everyone see my screen?"

CHAPTER 15

I'll Always Cheer For Wile E. Coyote

Wile E. Coyote is a mess. He looks like he gets about 45 minutes of sleep a night and hasn't had a warm meal in 10 years.

But what's interesting about Wile E., at least on paper, is he possesses a lot of the characteristics we normally view as strengths. He's incredibly creative. Never runs out of ideas. He's resilient. Persistent. Goal oriented. Not afraid to fail.

And he definitely fails a lot. But that's not a bad thing either. Failing is hot right now. Once a week, I'll see one of these three stories referenced on LinkedIn:

- Michael Jordan saying, "I failed, I missed so many game-winning shots."
- Abe Lincoln failed his way to the White House.
- Thomas Edison failed 10,000 times on the lightbulb but said, "I haven't failed, I just found 10,000 ways that would not work."

Maybe Wile E. just needs 10,001 attempts...

Wile E. doesn't spend time worrying about what others think of his Road Runner pursuit. When Elmer Fudd and Yosemite Sam are swapping war stories about their failed attempts at Bugs Bunny, the conversation always ends with, "Welp, at least we're not as pathetic as ol Wile E. I heard he doesn't even own a bar of soap."

But none of this bothers the disheveled coyote. He stays the course and tries again.

That's another one of his strengths: Wile E. isn't afraid to dream big AND he has a measurable goal.

The goal: I want to catch the Road Runner.

How will I know when I get there? I will have caught the Road Runner.

Pretty straightforward.

I think we should all have some ridiculous goals. Ones that feel kind of embarrassing to admit in public. For me, I want to write at least 20 books in my life. If the dream stays right there, that's a measurable goal. I'll know when I've hit 20. But if it drifts into, "I want to write the greatest novel ever" or "I want to be a famous author," now it's in the "How do I know when I get there?" fantasy land. And, once the goal drifts into that space, we either a) never get started, because it feels too daunting or b) struggle to enjoy the process or any of the small victories along the way because we're chasing this elusive, hard-to-measure finish line.

Success seems to make it all worth it though, right? We revere the people who go at it alone, obsess over a problem, then finally solve it. Like if someone locked themselves in a basement for 40 years and found the cure for cancer, their name would be remembered forever. No one would say, "Yeah, but isn't it kinda sad he never had any kids? He never went down a water slide with his family at The Wisconsin Dells."

But when characters like Wile E. Coyote or Captain Ahab have the obsession without a later victory, they are seen as the ultimate tragic characters.

It becomes a high stakes gamble to make:

Obsession + Success = Iconic Hero

Obsession - Success = Tragic Character

I wonder if the secret, then, is to avoid obsessing over a big goal. To not play this high-risk game of Hero vs. Tragic Character. To say, "Well, I might not become Thomas Edison, but at least I won't become Wile E. Coyote."

Instead, maybe the right alternative is to just have some reasonable, realistic goals. Build some healthy work/life balance. And when someone tells you to shoot for the stars, you reply, "Eh, I'm pretty good with the moon."

But I do have one major critique of Wile E. Coyote; one area I believe is holding him back. I mean let's break it down, he's dreaming big. Check. Not worrying what others think of him. Check. He's got a measurable goal. Check. Is the only thing that Wile E's doing wrong just being really bad at catching the Road Runner? And, if he finally does succeed, will we look at him differently? Will we suddenly view all of the failed attempts as these crucial moments of growth as he figured things out?

Maybe. But I think where Wile E. messed up is that in his obsession, he never asked anyone for help. If the absolute goal is catching the Road Runner, then why not bring in someone else for assistance? There's nothing wrong with Michael Jordan passing the ball to Steve Kerr for a big game-winning shot. Nothing wrong with Abe Lincoln having someone read over one of his speeches. Nothing wrong with Thomas Edison having an assistant in the lab. The goal in those scenarios was to win the NBA Title, deliver a great speech, invent the light bulb, not do it 100 percent alone. If Wile E. adds Elmer Fudd, Yosemite Sam, and Daffy Duck to his pursuit, they might all combine to be one somewhat effective character. Or what if he brought in an expert? What if he paid Bugs Bunny for some consulting advice? He could totally reach his goal of catching the Road Runner.

I don't think anyone has achieved a major accomplishment without some help or coaching from a friend, colleague, parent, teacher, etc. somewhere along the way. Even something as "solo" as writing a book isn't all that solo. I sent *Here or There* out to friends to review and help me with editing. I worked with an artist on the cartoons. Another artist on the cover design. Two marketing experts read over the back of the book description, made some key suggestions. The list goes on and on. Freelance help for the book formatting. Help with the grammar. I received help with everything. I'd be crazy to go at all of this alone. I never would have caught the Road Runner.

I don't want to end this chapter with, "Therefore, if Wile E. would have asked for help, if *we* ask for help, we will all succeed and live happily ever after. The End." There are no guarantees. It is still entirely possible that Wile E. Coyote will never catch the Road Runner.

But if he could say to himself, "You know what, I've tried as hard as I possibly can. I've put years into this quest. I've gotten all the help that I can, and it's STILL not working. Maybe this isn't the right calling for me," that's not a tragic ending at all. He would have the rest of his life to find a new pursuit. Or pursue the Road Runner as a casual hobby. He doesn't have to be great at it. There are plenty of golfers out there who shoot a triple bogey on a Par 3 and think to themselves, "Eh, I still love this game."

Instead, ol Wile E. is off in the desert right now, alone, strapping a rocket to his back, hoping this will be the time his plan finally works.

I wish him the best. I'll always cheer for Wile E. Coyote.

Wile E. Coyote Cheering Section

Chapter 16

Relaxed People Stress me Out

I was standing in line at the rental car place. The line was only about 20 people deep, but each couple took 15 minutes once they got to the front desk. Ashley was outside standing by the suitcases. I was inside on a mission to stay calm.

We had been in Italy for nine or ten days, so I was filled with that deep vacation chill. As slow as things were moving in line, it wasn't bothering me. I could do this all day.

Behind me was a couple fresh off of their flight. You could smell the jetlag. And the guy wasn't nearly as relaxed.

"This is ridiculous. How hard is it? You come to the desk, you say your name, look up the reservation, that's it. Let's go. Come on. Let's go."

His wife was decked out in standard yoga class attire. She stood next to him stretching, arms reaching up to the sky, twisting her back from side to side.

"Let's stay calm. They'll figure it out. See, the line will start moving any second now. Any second."

Couple seconds go by.

"Oh, come on. This is ridiculous. What other options are there? What about that place?"

The room had four or five other rental car companies. There were no lines in front of their counters.

"Honey, we looked that up, remember?" the wife said. "They're $300 or $400 more expensive. I mean you can check, but that's way too much."

"Yeah, well, at this pace it might be worth it."

Heavy sigh. Heavy sigh. This continued until the wife finally said, "Hey, I'm just trying to stay positive, alright?! Look, we're tired. This sucks. But there's nothing we can do about it. So, relax."

In that moment, I realized something: Relaxed people stress me out.

Because, when you have two people together, someone has to play the role of "Relaxed" and the other person plays the role of "Stressed." Or, a healthier way of looking at it: "In Control" and "Going with the Flow." Type A and Type B.

Type A's use words like "itinerary" and "logistics." Type B's use words like "nap." Type A's are always on a mission. Type B's are on a mission to not be on a mission. Type A's are the reason offices have a dress code policy. Type B's need the dress code policy so they don't show up to work in a swimsuit.

Rules, lists, and processes vs. "Eh, it'll all work itself out." Neither one is a better mindset (unless, of course, you are Type A then the answer is obviously Type A). It's not really a choice either, we naturally gravitate to one of the two options. If you're Type A, there's a constant checklist going on. *Do we have our tickets? Do we have the passports? What time is the flight?*

While this mental checklist is going on, the Type B partner is thinking, "I don't remember what we had for dinner last night."

Should you try to alternate? Should the "In Control" person switch and "Go with the flow?" Absolutely not! There's nothing more stressful for a Type A than turning the reigns over to a Type B. If Ashley put me in charge at the airport, we would end up on the next flight to Botswana.

Or look at a show like *The West Wing*. The President's staff is continuously stressed out so the President can remain calm. An hour before a big speech, the President wants to see his staff in a panic. Nothing would be more stressful than to walk in and everyone's relaxed playing Ping Pong.

In a group of two, only one person can be in charge. Have you ever seen two Type A's together? Both people want to lead. It's constant second-guessing. *Hmm. I wouldn't have done it that way. You turned left? Hmm. I would have gone right there, but hey, you're the boss, right?*

Or what about two Type B's together? They'll never leave the house! It turns into the vulture scene from Disney's *Jungle Book*. *Hey Flaps, what we gonna do? I don't know. Whatchu wanna do? I dunno. What about you?*

And the thing is, even if you have the two most chill people in the world together, in a relationship, at some point one of the two will take charge and establish themselves as the "Stressed" partner. Someone has to come up with the gameplan.

Since someone has to play each part, when you go back and review the jetlag situation from earlier—all of the stretching, the gentle voice, the let's relax—that is actually forcing the other person to play the role of Stressed. Had she been the one complaining about the line, he would have gotten to be the Relaxed yoga guy.

Take it a step further, I think this is why our customer service policies are completely backward. We train people on the phones, behind the counter, at the front desk to stay calm at all costs. Never get upset. Just peacefully say, "I hear you, and I understand you're upset. We're doing everything we can. Thank you for your patience." This doesn't calm down the customer. Far from it! When you hear that over the phone, you can just picture the guy chewing gum and scrolling through his Instagram page.

No, I want the customer service rep to show up sweating. Like you know how there's always that one guy at a Home Depot who looks totally stressed out? His apron is covered in grease. His hands look like they just wrestled a charcoal grill. That's the best guy on staff! You ask for help, they wipe their arm across their brow, let out a big sigh. "I'm working on it, alright!?" They catch their breath. Run their hand over their face. "Sorry. Try aisle seven." Now *that* is customer service. When this guy says he's doing everything he can, I 100 percent believe him. By fulfilling the role of Stressed, the customer is then able to relax.

I finally reached the front of the line. Got the keys, got the rental car. I handed the receipt over to my Type A wife. She looked it over and, as expected, I totally Type B'd the transaction. Paid $130 extra so we could return the car without a full tank of gas.

"We'll worry about it later," Ashley said with a sigh. "Let's go."

My first drive overseas involved climbing up a cliff to reach our hotel in Cinque Terre. Now, this wasn't a full out *Fear Factor* one lane and no guard rail type of experience, but it was still pretty intense. As we rounded the turns, we could look down and see just how high we were (more intense from where Ashley was sitting in the passenger seat). We were both trying not to have that, "Shrek, I'm looooking down!" moment.

Because of her seat, and because she knew there was a Type B behind the wheel (who was probably thinking more about writing this chapter than he was about the actual drive), Ashley was, naturally, feeling pretty stressed out. Taking deep breaths. Avoiding the views over the guard rail.

Let's just get there. Four more miles. Almost there. Almost there. Get me out of here.

In this moment, as she was absorbing all of the anxiety in the automobile, I felt completely calm. Not because I have nerves of steel. Far from it. But, because Ashley took on the role of Stressed, I could be relaxed.

We need each other. Type A's need Type B's to help get out of their head. Type B's need Type A's to help stay alive.

I think my dad says it best:

"Type B's are like balloons floating in the sky; we need a Type A holding onto the string. Otherwise, we would just kind of float away."

Imposter Syndrome

Patient: I think I'm suffering from imposter syndrome.
Therapist: Great. Now can I have my chair back?

CHAPTER 17

Virginia Woolf Kicked the Crap out of Me

Outside, the Western Michigan snow was piled high. A brutal winter was in full force, and it was always dark out. I don't think I had seen the sun in three weeks and I'm not sure if I'm even exaggerating.

But the snow was nothing compared to the opponent I would face that winter. A woman whose name I will surely never forget.

Virginia Woolf. She could not have weighed more than 110 lbs, and I'm not sure she has ever thrown a punch. But man, back in January of 2009, I was more afraid of her than an actual wolf. She put a new spin on the old schoolyard phrase: sticks and stones may break my bones. With Virginia, it was, "Sticks and stones may break my bones, but words, they just might kill me."

The book we were assigned was *Mrs. Dalloway*. You know how some books are labeled as the "perfect beach read?" Well, *Mrs. Dalloway* is the perfect "winter beach read," you know, when you go to the same beach on a zero-degree day, sit down naked and cry.

Mrs. Dalloway is filled with uplifting, flowery quotes like:

It might be possible that the world itself is without meaning.

Or:

She always had the feeling that it was very, very dangerous to live even one day.

Virginia Woolf was opening up some pitch-black doors, taking me on a journey through the most depressing thoughts imaginable. I'm not sure why I kept on reading. It was probably some built-in Disney movie programming, assuming things would turn around. I mean, the mom dies in *Finding Nemo*, Mufasa in *Lion King*, or how about that painfully sad opening of *Up*. I figured *Mrs. Dalloway* would be like that. Things had to get better... *right?*

Something worth mentioning, Virginia Woolf is an incredible writer. So yes, this book was painful to read, but not in a six percent Rotten Tomatoes sort of way. It was painful because here was a master of writing choosing to focus on PTSD and depression as her main subjects. With all of that skill comes terrifying accuracy, and with that accuracy comes a great deal of discomfort for the reader.

When we finished the book, we watched a film adaptation called *The Hours*. That back-to-back combination is kind of like putting your dog down in the morning then heading to a funeral in the afternoon.

The Hours is about three women who are tied together by the book *Mrs. Dalloway*. The film opens with Virginia Woolf (played by Nicole Kidman) walking into a river, writing and reading off her suicide note. Another character kills himself in the film. A third character, Laura, almost does as well, but ultimately decides not to. It's basically a two-hour film about suicide.

Class ended and I remember walking outside feeling devastated. I knew I wanted to be a writer; I had known that since second grade, but all I could think about was that movie, and how Virginia Woolf killed herself, Ernest Hemingway - same thing, David Foster Wallace - same thing. It was like, ok, odds are really low that you can ever make it as a writer, and then, even if you do, look at how it ended for these three famous authors. And that's *with* success. It was a terrible thought to wrestle with.

And there was no Timon and Pumbaa singing *Hakuna Matata*. I didn't have Dory singing *Just Keep Swimming*. No, I had *The Hours*, and *Mrs. Dalloway*, and another dark, cold, snowy day. I couldn't even chuckle at the irony of walking by the campus sign that read: "Hope College" covered under a foot of snow.

But the day wasn't finished. I had one more movie to see that would heap on another layer of melancholia. I went with my class to see the movie *Pray the Devil Back to Hell*. It's a ~~nice romantic comedy with Paul Rudd~~ heavy movie about Christian and Muslim women coming together, starting a peace movement in response to a civil war in Liberia that "left hundreds of thousands of people dead or displaced." Overall, it was inspiring, but all I could see was the civil war aspect. The death. The tragedy. The snow was piling higher on my bleak worldview.

I remember crawling (metaphorically, but maybe literally too) into my dorm room, laying down on my bed, and feeling worse than any high school basketball loss, or whatever else I could try and compare this day to from a pretty sheltered, easy, Midwestern life.

The lousy day ended, and the sun rose again (or at least I think it did, somewhere behind the clouds). Life went on. A week later, the book and the movie felt further away. A month later, my black eye from Virginia Woolf had pretty much healed.

And now, ten years later, I find it all pretty funny to look back on. I think how soft my skin must have been. Like imagine one of those women in Liberia: *Oh Chris, here, please take a seat. Tell me about how depressed you felt after reading that book. That must have been so hard on you! I mean this Civil War, sure, I've seen family members die, but Virginia Woolf sounds way more intense. Tell me about that 36-hour car alarm too.*

But hey, this was my starting point. A 19-year-old kid being exposed to some pretty heavy stuff. And there'd be other tough topics over the next few years of college. Not necessarily as or more depressing, but other intellectual challenges. For example, I'm a Christian, went to a Christian college, but we were assigned to read Sam Harris and Richard Dawkins. I heard intelligent, well-researched arguments against my beliefs. I had to come up with my own answers.

And sure, it was tough. These brought up doubts, challenged me, pushed me to think critically. Forced me to defend my positions. Forced me to grow. That's what college should be about.

And you mix that with kegs, and parties, and late-night runs to Taco Bell. Or that midnight run to Long John Silver's as a fraternity pledge, sitting in the backseat talking like a drunken pirate. You mix that with going to chapel services (or running naked around the chapel after midnight). You write a column in the school newspaper about how bad the campus food is, get a bunch of laughs, except for a cafeteria worker who was really hurt by what you wrote. And you feel that guilt, truly feel it, and sincerely apologize, realizing that jokes can have consequences, and are more careful next time around.

But you don't give up on writing. Or telling jokes. Absolutely not. Go up on stage, tell a joke about crying in the shower while peeling a clementine. Keep writing, keep reading, keep scrambling to finish Spanish homework an hour before it's due. Meet a girl, fall in love, go off to New York City for a semester, learn what it's like to be over 500 miles away from home, and realize it's not that scary after all. Learn that some lessons came in the classroom, but most are delivered outside of it. Life rarely teaches behind a podium.

Get to the end of those four years and wonder, man, where did all the time go? Look at the new freshman class walking around campus. They look younger than I remember being. Maybe they just got assigned *Mrs. Dalloway* for Freshman English, but right now, who cares. There's music playing at a fraternity house. There's a football game at noon. There's a big test coming up that feels like it will determine your entire future until you get to the future and wonder, "Why was I so worried about that test?"

Pass by the Hope College sign wearing your cap and gown. It's the first week of May. The snow has melted. The tulips are in full bloom. Four years went by in the blink of an eye. You look back at the campus and smile with a new sense of confidence.

"Who's afraid of Virginia Woolf?"

The Halfway Point

Patient: Doc, I think I'm having a quarter-life crisis.
Doctor: Good news, you're not. Bad news, it's more of a midlife.

Chapter 18

Farewell, LOL

It was 9 o'clock on a Monday night, and I was determined not to get caught. I tip-toed down the hallway avoiding any creaky step. I made the turn into my parents' computer room, sat down in the office chair, took a deep breath. I was about to do what all 12-year-old boys do...

Log on to AOL Instant Messenger.

I clicked on the AOL icon and crossed my fingers.

The screen showed three boxes. The furthest to the left had the little yellow running man. The next two boxes were empty. The objective was to get the running man over to the right, and it was no easy task. The word "dialing" popped up and you heard this quick *beep-bop-beep-bop-boop* sound of someone placing a phone call.

From there, all hell breaks loose. The sound was this combination of someone putting their car keys in a blender mixed with the cries of a kitten. You immediately cringe.

Come on, come on! Go-go-go-go!

There's no way to turn off the sound. And it was LOUD. It was not just a risk for my parents to hear, I think people down the street were asking, "Hey, is somebody logging on AOL?"

After about thirty seconds, an amount of time that felt like 30 days, the running man gets to the second box then quickly finishes his journey getting to the third. *Dude, where was that late burst of speed at the beginning??*

My AIM buddy list pops up. I'm officially online. But it doesn't matter. Mom comes by, "Chris, sign off. It's time for bed."

At some point, every generation starts to say, "You kids don't know how good you have it." But for each generation, the referenced struggle gets a little bit softer.

My grandpa could say, "Kid, I had to fight in World War 2."

My parents could say, "Boy, we never had romaine lettuce."

My generation? "When we were kids, there was no such thing as WiFi."

But, at the time, AOL still seemed impressive. You'd log on, have five different AOL Instant Messages (AIM) going all at once. The language was different too, we all had our own tween and teen lingo. *G2G. BRB. OMG.*

The most confusing was "POS." Parent over shoulder. Was the rule in that household, "Sweetie, you can go online for 15 minutes, but I will stand behind you like a member of the Secret Service."

There were plenty of other acronyms; some that still show up in text messages today, others that would require a little bit of Wikipedia research.

But the one that needs no introduction at all, the absolute rockstar of the batch was "LOL."

LOL was a dominant force from 1998 to 2003. I'd say one out of every 3.5 messages on AIM had an LOL in it. It quickly became a part of American culture, and I assume it's even included in Webster's dictionary.

LOL and AIM were linked together. They were like Brady and Belichick or Trump and Twitter. As LOL did well, so did AIM. AIM was as popular during its heyday—at least with the under 18 crowd—as Snap, Instagram, and TikTok are today.

But the value of the LOL currency started to plummet, kind of like what we're seeing today with exclamation points. LOL became cheap. Anything from a bad pun to a legitimately hilarious story was met with the same response: "LOL."

And that wasn't ok because, realistically, not every joke gets a laugh out loud. Some jokes deserve a light chuckle. Some get one of those weird nose breaths. I remember we all started clarifying the level of laugh. People would use capitals (LOL) when a joke deserved more respect. We introduced "Literally Laughing Out Loud" (LLOL) or, the most extreme, "ROFL" as in "Rolling on Floor Laughing." Anytime I received a "ROFL" I was like, thank you, I'm honored, but are you sure you're ok? Should I call for help?

It also became hard as a guy to use LOL. And I know in 2019 it's dangerous to label anything as feminine or masculine but, for what it's worth (FWIW), which of these scenes feels out of place:

Group of women at a book club, Sheila tells a joke, Amy responds, "LOL, that's hilarious."

Group of men in the coal mine, Steve tells a joke, Al responds, "LOL, now could you pass me the pickaxe?"

As men (insert Tim Allen grunt), we pivoted to the ultra-manly "haha" instead. But that didn't really convey a real laugh. Sounded robotic. *Hi. I enjoyed that joke very much. Ha. Haha. Ha. Ha. Ha.*

So, you'd start to see "hahah" get thrown out there, that extra 'h' showing this was a more serious moment of laughter.

As text conversations moved away from the computer and onto smartphones, there was new competition. Enter the emojis. Ever since 2008, LOL's biggest opponent is not another acronym; it's that laughing while crying smiley face.

Emojis introduced this new idea: Why use words, why use letters at all when we can use smiley faces?

Or, as we found out on September 12, 2017, Apple was ready to take us one step further. Apple posed the question: Why use emojis when you could use an *animoji?*

I watched Craig Federighi, Senior Vice President of Engineering at Apple, a dude whose net worth is north of $150 million, stand on stage and bock like a chicken. He displayed how you could turn your face into a chicken, a dog, or the infamous poop emoji. As I watched this, I thought, "Yep. This is the beginning of the end."

Off in the distance, I heard someone start to softly play *American Pie* on their guitar.

Oh, and as I watched him on the stage
My hands were clenched in fists of rage
No angel born in Hell
Could break that iPhone's spell

I don't think it's a coincidence that not even a month after the animoji announcement, AOL threw their hands up in the air—we can't compete with this—and announced that AOL Instant Messenger was officially calling it a career. Retiring after twenty years of service. The yellow running guy would move on to the fourth box, the internet afterlife; go live alongside Myspace and The Hampster Dance.

The *American Pie* music grew louder in the background.

It became clear to me what I needed to do. AIM and LOL started together, it's only right for them to end together. So, I have decided I've sent my final LOL. It's time for LOL to RIP.

And I know, LOL will still exist. It will kick around for a few more years, but I want to end it now with dignity. I don't want to see LOL struggle like a 40-year-old NBA player trying to run up and down the court against emojis and animojis and whatever else comes next. I don't want to see LOL go out weak and defeated.

It's time. LOL, you were a valuable part of our childhoods, an integral part of 21st-century culture. You are as American as apple pie, and you served us well. But all things must pass. With a heavy heart I say, LOL, it's time to face the music.

I went down to the sacred store
Where I'd heard the dial-tones play before
But the man there said the dial-tones wouldn't play

And in the Tweets, the children screamed
The lovers cried, and the poets dreamed
But no more AIMs were written
No sounds of that dial-tone kitten

And the two things I admire most
An LOL in an IM post
They caught the last train for the coast
The day, AIM died

And they were singing...

Bye, bye yellow running man guy
Plugged my modem to the phone line but the dial tones were dry
That running guy was drinking whiskey and rye
Singin' this'll be the day that I die

There are few moments more vulnerable than when someone overhears you asking Siri to type LOL

Chapter 19

The Escalator Dictator

I try to respect every form of commuter. Everyone from the, "I still need space to read my Kindle on a crowded train" to the, "I just want to let everybody know, I will be sneezing all over the place." These are my fellow Chicagoans. We are all trying to survive the morning commute.

Where I lose this friendly, "we're all in this together" attitude is with the Escalator Dictator. This is a tyrant who is not so much a person but an ideology that has taken over El stops, malls, theaters, sporting arenas, you name it. Wherever there is an escalator, you can find an Escalator Dictator filling the air with a chorus of sighs because, heaven forbid, one guy in front would like to take 30 seconds to stand still. The Escalator Dictator is determined to speed things up. They want to turn the escalator into a staircase.

No place in Chicago is this pressure higher than at the North and Clybourn Red Line stop. See, most escalators are just wide enough to set up like the people movers at airports with a clear walking lane on the left, standing lane on the right. This allows the Escalator Dictator to push their way up the left side, smacking people's calves with their suitcase, breathing out sharp, *"Excuse me. Ex-CUSE me"* marching orders.

But at North and Clybourn, it's truly one lane. There is no way to get around a standing rider.

When I choose to stand still, it sets off a chain reaction of sighs. I turn around. Everyone has that stuck on the highway look, craning their neck to the side, seeing if there was a crash ahead that's holding up traffic. *What's the problem here? Move!*

My noble stand lasts about five seconds. I want to hold my ground longer, see if I start getting booed, but the pressure of the sighs is too much. I cave to the Escalator Dictator.

What I don't understand is the motivation of the Escalator Dictator. If you want to move faster, that's fine, more power to you, but why not use the stairs? They are right there! Do whatever you want on the stairs. Run. Do lunges. Pretend you're Rocky Balboa. More power to you.

But the person who walks up the escalator is like the guy who goes into the stall, stands and pees with the door wide open. Why are you not at the urinal? If you're in the stall, close the door, sit down, scroll through the phone, and relax. Or it's like a group of adults saying, "Hey, wanna go play basketball?" and the dictator replies, "No, I'm alright," then heads over to the local elementary school to dunk on fourth graders. There shouldn't be anything to prove on the escalator. You don't win an award for being the fastest one to the top.

Instead, the escalator should be an escape; a much-needed sanctuary from an otherwise hectic morning. Think about the entire mindset of a random Tuesday. It starts with our peaceful sleep being interrupted by a beeping alarm clock. Then it's off to the races. Shower. Put in your contacts. Brush your teeth. The dog has to go out. Kids have to be woken up. Get everyone off to school.

And what do you eat for breakfast? No matter which option you pick, there is somebody out there making the argument that it will kill you. French toast, pancakes, waffles. *Too much sugar, you'll die.* Cereal, muffins, donuts. *Death.* Orange juice. *Death by citrus.* Alright, I'll make some eggs. *Well, scientists say eggs are either secretly good for you or possibly worse than smoking.* Ok, then I'll have this protein bar. Eh, too many carbs. Alright, fine, I'll just have a coffee. *Well, coffee is either great for your brain or a borderline cocaine addiction.*

From there, everything's a race to be on time. On time for the bus. On time for the train. On time for work. When we're not thinking about being late, we distract ourselves on the phone with some articles, a couple Facebook/Instagram scrolls, a look at the work email. Everything is to pass the time. Even the people on the bus sitting there calmly reading a physical book, it's still a way to escape the current moment. There is only like one person on the bus gazing out the window, peacefully living in the moment. And that's because they hit their Happiness Deductible back in January.

When we get to the escalator, that's our moment to just be. It's the rare moment in life where we can stand motionless and still move forward. Why rush through that experience?

I don't only advocate for standing still on the escalator, I think we should go full airplane mode. No scrolling through the phone. No thoughts about work. No email. This is our opportunity to slow down and observe the surroundings. To have a song stuck in our head.

Everything before the escalator and everything after is chaotic, hurried, and filled with decision making. So, let's take a few seconds to stand still and relax. We'll still reach the top and the stress can return right after the escalator ride.

There's nothing wrong with living in the moment.

The final days of a non-stick pan are just a very sticky pan

CHAPTER 20

But Maybe "Living in the Moment" Is Overrated

The Florentine Steak (on the menu as the Bistecca) is a giant cut of meat. A massive t-bone. You pick the size by the kilogram, but when I say pick the size, it's like walking into a Big and Tall store and deciding between XL, Double XL, and Shaquille O'Neal. Websites say it's served medium rare (which makes me an immediate fan), but I think that's an exaggeration. It's hard to say that this steak is anything other than rare.

But it's not the rare of a steak at a U.S. diner that tastes like they pulled it out of the freezer, threw it on a frying pan for a couple of seconds, and said, "Alright, here you go." It's a different experience. The outer part is still really hot, and the middle is room temperature. Maybe even a little bit colder than that. The seasoning is incredibly simple, just salt and pepper. Three bites in, I already declared that this was the best steak I'd ever eaten.

Then I found out I was doing it all wrong. The waiter came by, doused the steak in olive oil. "Here, try it now." I took a bite. *Woah.* That took it up a notch. The olive oil brings out even more of the flavors, and I wish I had the palate of like a *New York Times* food critic to describe what I was tasting, but all I can say is: that steak was awesome. It was the best steak on the planet, and that was even before I knew how to eat it right!

In the end, the waiter returned and encouraged me to pick up the steak, bite into it as if it were a rack of ribs. I'm still about a 50/50 split if this was an honest recommendation or a trick to play on the gullible American. Either way, I gladly walked right into it.

We came. We saw. We ate half a cow.

Sitting at the table next to us was a nice couple, probably about 10 years older and significantly less caveman than me. Toward the end of the meal, the husband and wife leaned over and asked, "So, where are you guys from?" This sort of greeting happens at almost every dinner on vacation, which is fine, but sometimes you just want to reply, "Sorry, can we not do this tonight."

When the couple asked what we had seen so far, I told them about that first moment seeing the Cathedral and the Duomo and how amazing it was that something with that much hype could—not only live up to it—but exceed it. They nodded their heads in agreement. When they asked if we had gone to the Uffizi Gallery, we decided not to sugar coat it, we just gave them our honest take.

"I hate to say it, but we were museum-ed out by that point. We walked through there and were like, 'Ok, I know these are important pieces, but we were just so tired.'"

"Oh, for sure! We had that too!"

"And finding the exit, it was like a mile walk to get out of there. We were trapped!"

"Right?! Totally with you. That's so funny, we literally said the same thing."

The most connected we felt to any strangers on the entire trip was in this moment, bonding over a mutual sucky story, not a positive one. The retelling of the Duomo got a couple of head nods. The retelling of Uffizi created an immediate bond.

When we say "live in the moment," it usually carries with it a positive connotation. The "live in the moment" advice is almost always paired with a glass-half-full lens. Take the Uffizi Gallery example. When we were there, the "in the moment" thing to have done is to say, "I know I'm tired right now, but I need to count my blessings. I need to realize what an incredible opportunity this is."

But I'd argue the actual "in the moment" experience, the honest one, the one you don't have to meditate your way into, works out much better. If you're feeling fatigued and grouchy, let that be the moment. If you're thinking, "Wow, that's it?" then that's the moment. Let it be what it is.

There is this extra pressure on a vacation, especially when you are looking at a famous site (or sight) to "get in the moment." A pressure to have this almost out-of-body religious experience while you're over There. But I'd argue that those types of moments come naturally and can't be forced. The Duomo, I didn't have to think my way into. The Florentine steak, just look at that description above. I remember every little detail, and I do because I was completely in the moment during that dinner. At no point mid-bite did I think, "Ok, Chris, let's really try and focus here. Let's capture just how much I'm enjoying this."

When you're in the moment, you're not thinking about it. Like if you're working hard on a project you love, once you've entered that state of flow, the quickest way to end it is to think, "Wow, I'm really in the zone right now." Nope. Zone over. You've lost the state of flow.

In the words of Deepak Chopra:

"The best way to be in the present moment is to be aware that you're NOT in the moment. As soon as you're aware that you're NOT in the moment, you're in the moment."

Or, said even simpler by former Boston Celtics big man Glen "Big Baby" Davis.

"Let me tell you something right quick. When ya in the moment, ya in the moment."

Those incredible "in the moment" experiences that we search for on a vacation, or life in general, will come naturally and be stored away in the memory forever. And the disappointments where we couldn't "get in the moment," well, those don't need to be anything else. They end up making surprisingly good stories, ones that almost everyone can relate to.

As I've been writing about Florence, I already feel it being elevated into that sacred, romantic part of the memory where everything wears the "Best Ever" label. Best year ever. Best show ever. Best trip ever. It's easy to remember all of the good stuff.

But what I don't recall quite as fast is the part when we got to our hotel for the first time, and I needed to carry our suitcases up two massive flights of stairs. Our suitcases were packed to capacity. Had to be fifty pounds apiece. For me and my skinny arms, this workout felt somewhere in between being an NFL player flipping one of those giant tires and going through the first day of Marines boot camp. Add in the creepiness factor, the whole Stephen King vibe to the main entrance and how it felt like Dracula might pop out at any moment and bite me right in the neck. I'm pretty sure organ music was playing, and I passed by those two twin girls from *The Shining*.

Two months later, the staircase memory doesn't come to mind because it doesn't fit the overall "Florence is amazing" narrative. My brain has decided that everything about Florence is incredible, so the P90x: Staircase Edition, or our lackluster trip through the Uffizi Gallery, are pushed away in favor of all the positive memories. The same thing happened with college. Same thing with senior year of high school. Same thing with shows like *Friday Night Lights*, *Breaking Bad*, *Seinfeld*; it's a lot easier to remember the best episodes than recall any of the average ones.

But that's not the same for, let's say, middle school. Since the overall story of middle school is focused on how awkward and uncomfortable life was for those three years, all of the memories that stand out are ones that support this general theme. So, I remember the acne, the puberty, the voice cracks. Any embarrassing memory goes right to the front of the line. Anything positive, the bouncer puts out his arm, "Woah, easy there. The club's full."

The truth is, there were good memories from sixth to eighth grade. Plenty of good dinners, plenty of laughs. But those are harder to access. It's the reverse situation of the Florence trip. When looking back on middle school, everything feels like it was one giant staircase climb.

Daniel Gilbert's book *Stumbling on Happiness* dives into this concept more, explaining how our memory edits and groups things together. His overall idea is paraphrased like this:

Our memories aren't supercomputers. Unless we are like Dustin Hoffman's character in *Rainman*, our minds are not able to have a file for each and every day that we can easily access at any given moment. Instead, as we accumulate 30, 50, 80 years of life, we need an easier way to separate things out. So, our brain starts building a bookshelf. Four years of high school becomes one book. College, same thing. Middle school, same (it's just listed in the Horror section).

As each book gets assigned a theme, the memories fall into line, not the other way around. For example, growing up, my family and I would go on two-week sailing vacations along Lake Huron. I did this from age seven to 15 or 16-years-old. Now, years later, I idolize these trips. I think how cool it would be to take two weeks off of work and sail from Bay City to Mackinaw Island again. To see the North Channel again. To stop by that pizza place in Tawas, Michigan.

But if you went back and asked 13-year-old "in the moment" Chris if he loved that year's specific sailing vacation, that little fricker would say no. He would complain how boring those 12-hour sailing journeys from town to town were. How he wished he didn't lose two weeks of his summer vacation each year. How he spent more time looking at the Nintendo Gameboy than looking outside at the water. THAT would be the true, in-the-moment answer.

But when I bring this memory to the little editor in the memory room, he simply looks it over and says, "Nah. Delete that. We're going with the awesome pizza place instead. This 'Sailing' book is a happy one. Put those negative scenes in the middle school book."

It creates a funny cycle, because the edited memory, jam-packed with all of the positive nostalgia, could lead me to buy a sailboat later on in life. And then I'll be frustrated at my 13-year-old kid who is spending all of their time playing video games down below. *How could you not be up here enjoying this!?* Forgetting that I did the exact same thing.

Little bit different example is January during my freshman year of college. It was a horrible time. "In the moment" Chris would not have said anything positive about those long 31 days. He'd be sitting there on the couch in his ratty sweatpants saying, "Yeah, this place sucks. Virginia Woolf just beat the crap out of me."

But here's the other trick our memory pulls on us: if it can't edit out the bad parts, it transforms them into the all-important "adversity" chapters. So, while the "Sailing" book is all happy, no bad parts allowed, the "College" book follows more of a Disney movie format. "January of Freshman Year" serves as the Mufasa death scene. From there, it's the hero's journey, pretty much all positives complete with the typical happily ever after ending.

It's very hard for us to keep anything in our memory labeled as a tragedy. We don't keep many *Hamlets* or *Romeo and Juliets* on the shelves. Back to *Stumbling on Happiness*, the author points out that even the most serious examples (a death, a break-up/divorce, serious illness) even these, over time will develop—maybe not a happy ending—but at least a hopeful conclusion.

Now, there are definitely exceptions, some events that have no other path than remaining a tragedy, but here's how the memory editor might translate the following three events:

Death of a loved one - I'm glad they were in my life. They taught me how to be a better son/daughter/parent/friend.

Break-up/divorce - They weren't the right person for me, I'm much happier to be with so-and-so now.

Serious Illness - It taught me to live a more fulfilling life, to cherish every moment.

But if you don't end up cherishing every moment, no worries, because your memory will do the sorting for you. This is why, just a chapter after making my case for standing still on the escalator, I think I've convinced myself that living in the moment is secretly overrated.

Because...

- If the moment is incredible, you will naturally remember every little detail and be so in the flow that you won't be thinking about capturing it. You'll just simply be "in the moment."
- If the moment is mundane or average, the memory will edit it out.
- If the moment is negative, the memory will either edit it out or re-purpose it as adversity in a bigger story.

Therefore, it doesn't matter if you have your phone out or not when riding an escalator, because every escalator ride gets edited out anyways as a mundane moment. Something really significant would have to happen for it to be worth remembering.

So, what should we do with the other stuff? How should we handle the moments that are neither "best ever" or "worst ever?"

I think the answer is that we should take a bunch of photos. Record a ton of videos. Write things down. Feed as much material as possible to the internal memory, and let the internal editor do the sorting. "Capture the moment" can become our new updated slogan.

And, in 20 years, I will have forgotten all of this. Ashley and I will be at the pizza place in Tawas, Michigan and a couple will ask us, "Hey, we're planning a trip to Florence, do you think we should take a tour of this place called the Uffizi Gallery?" We may tell them the disappointing truth but more likely we'll reply, "Oh, you've gotta go there. It's incredible. Everything about Florence is incredible." We'll leave the restaurant, head back to the sailboat daydreaming about the sunsets, the steak, the gelato, and we'll look over to see our 13-year-old daughter texting and taking selfies the entire time. I'll let out a sigh and say:

"Florence, you really need to start living in the moment."

In fifty years, *Turn Down for What* will be played at a wedding and we will all rush out to the dance floor. The kids will watch and ask each other, "How do they dance to this music?"

CHAPTER 21

Winter is About Lowering Your Expectations

If I could describe the Midwest's complicated relationship with winter in one image, it would be a shirtless guy at a Cleveland Browns game. He's wearing one of those iconic dog masks, has a hot dog in hand, and a letter painted on his now-turning-purple stomach. The team could be 1-14, and this game has no playoff implications whatsoever, but it doesn't matter. Going to this game shirtless is all about being one with winter (and going home with a little bit of frostbite on the nipples).

We even encourage winter to "bring it on" from December 15 to New Year's Eve. We want snow on Christmas morning. We're crushed if we don't get it. Have you ever seen people in Michigan or Indiana on a Christmas Day without snow?

What's wrong, Dad? Didn't you get everything you asked for?

Yeah, almost everything...

December, January, February, that's winter at the height of its powers. Winter is showing off at that point, smacking home runs out of the stadium, cracking windshields. And we're right there cheering winter on. Not just the snow on Christmas morning thing, we want to experience all of our winter sports. We want to go skiing and snowmobiling. We want to sit outside with a flask of whiskey. We want to prove to our wives why the hot tub was a reasonable $4,000 investment.

Usually, winter starts to run out of steam by mid-March. That's why some of the heaviest snows of the season take place after St. Patrick's Day; it's winter saying, "Hey, this is probably my last shot of the year, so you better believe I'm going out with a bang."

After all of those cold and snowy months, there is nothing better than June and July in the Midwest. Those summer nights with the sun still out at 9, 9:30 at night, it makes you forget about winter altogether.

But the summer months breeze by fast. Temperatures start to drop in September. The days get shorter. The first snow can fall as early as late October, and we're right there again. Like the character Catherine from the Midwestern board room, I'm left wondering, "What am I doing here? Why do I keep doing this winter thing for six, seven months of the year?"

It was in one of these moments a few years ago when I made a very simple decision. I sat down and decided, "Alright, I'm going to LIKE winter now. I can't dislike a season that runs for half of the year."

I tried to figure out, ok, how am I going to like winter? The first step was having the right gear. You have to go all in on the coat. Have to buy some thick socks. Have to order some long underwear from Vermont (go with a new pair, there is no price point where a used pair of longjohns ever makes sense). After that, my strategy was pretty simple. I didn't need to get into snowboarding. I didn't need to watch YouTube videos of ice fishing. I didn't have to buy a pair of cross-country skis. All I did to start enjoying winter was to embrace the type of Friday nights I've always wanted to have.

My ideal Friday night is simple. Leave work, head right to the grocery store. High schoolers are grabbing Red Bulls; college kids are loading up on handles of cheap vodka. I pass by both of them and head to the adult cooler. *Ah, look at all that milk.* Grab the 2%, flip a coin between Chips Ahoy vs. Oreos, and then I am home free.

There is a certain level of pride on the walk home with the grocery bag full of milk, cookies, and a Digiorno. A group of girls walks by in short dresses, guys behind them in button-down shirts. No coats. They stand outside shivering, waiting for their Ubers. They are absolutely freezing. The only thing frozen about my night is the Digiorno pizza.

I open the door to our condo, throw on some sweatpants, hop under a blanket with Ashley.

When it's nice outside, my desire to come home and watch Netflix makes me feel guilty. I have the voice of my parents from all those boating vacations saying, "You're gonna waste a perfectly good summer night and stay inside?" But in the winter, no guilt whatsoever.

The secret to embracing winter isn't about battling the cold. You don't want to be like those young twenty somethings bouncing up and down outside. That's called being in denial. They're pretending they live in Laguna Beach. No, the secret to winter is all about lowering your expectations.

See, the summer is like an energetic puppy. It needs to be taken outside and walked. Right when you settle down on the couch, the puppy comes over with a tennis ball in its mouth, begging for some more outdoor play time.

The winter is like an overweight bulldog, he's content just sleeping on the floor.

Summer nights come with tequila shots at the hot new bar. Winter nights come with Keurig shots of hot cocoa. Summer nights start at 10:30 p.m. Winter nights, 10:30 is when Netflix asks, "Are you still watching?" Summer nights, I need to shower before going out. Winter nights, I should probably at least shower once before heading into work on Monday.

Summer is the one who is never satisfied. Demanding you dress up, requiring you to go out and make memories. *Come on, let's go to the beach! YOLO! Instagram!*

Winter will only occasionally slip you a cross country skiing coupon and if you say no, it's no big deal. Winter understands.

So, next time when winter stretches the snowfall into May or begins to lower the temperatures in late September, I say we also lower our expectations.

Don't ask a lot out of winter, because winter never asked a lot out of us.

The Polar Vortex

CHAPTER 22

How to Avoid Playing on The Work League Softball Team

Career advice columns will always suggest getting involved at work, both in and outside of the office. In the summertime, slow pitch softball is one way to do this, and that's great if you're the Derek Jeter, Jennie Finch, or Bryce Harper at the company.

But what if you are terrible at slow pitch softball? How can you tell your colleagues "No" without letting them down?

The natural solution here seems like a simple no thank you when the email sign-up goes around. The problem, though, is you might have a great quarter at your job, but last night your work rival hit a grand slam in the bottom of the ninth and was carried off the field on the shoulders of the CEO.

Not joining can make it seem like you are not a team player. You are not willing to scrape your knee for the good of the company. Plus, you're missing out on all of those celebratory trips to McDonald's.

With all of this stress in mind, here are three Medium Rare pieces of advice on how to politely avoid playing on the work league softball team; all without tarnishing your work reputation. (You can also use this advice for church league softball).

The Addition by Subtraction Narrative

When asked if you want to join, reply by saying, "I am so bad that the biggest contribution I can make is by NOT being on the team."

They will laugh and say, "Oh, come on, it's no pressure. All for fun. Really just an excuse to drink beer on a weeknight."

At this point, smile and say you'll think about it. Then conveniently go on vacation when final registration is due.

The Bad Lower Back Approach

Everyone respects a bad back. It's a sign of wisdom like gray hair or ordering escargot. But, unlike a made-up leg injury, you don't have to ham it up in the office limping around to show that you are still injured. With a bad back, people will understand that everyday life doesn't upset it, but the abrupt swinging motion in softball is not healthy on the vertebrae.

If your co-workers need further proof, then go to your doctor and get a note. Doctors are not supposed to write fake prescriptions; that lands them in a lot of trouble. However, you are not asking them to write an order for anything. Just a note that says, "Bad back."

There is no scenario in which the doctor can get in trouble for this. If the case goes to court, the jury will sympathize. *You mean my doctor can get me off the softball team too?? Not guilty! Pssst, Doc, do you have a second?*

Be the Stat Guru

Say no to joining the team, but offer to keep track of stats at the games.

This way, you are still a team player, and you get extra credit for sacrificing your valuable out of office time. This is a great career move, especially if your job is related to finance, math, spreadsheets, and/or accounting.

Your co-workers will all want to see their batting averages. Your boss will want to see how everyone is doing. You may be asked to give a weekly presentation with the ESPN theme music playing as an intro.

Throw in some fancy graphs and don't be surprised when you see a promotion come your way by season's end.

Or at least like a $25 gift card to McDonald's.

Modern Office

I was promised a standing desk...

CHAPTER 23

Check Your Font Size, Bro

I glanced at my older brother's phone, and it looked like he was reading from a large print *Reader's Digest*. Everything was zoomed in. The app buttons were bigger. His text messages—if the standard font size is 12 pt—looked like they were 18, maybe even 20.

Which was surprising to see, because my brother is the only one in my immediate family who doesn't have some form of glasses or contacts. He has, by all accounts, 20/20 vision. He doesn't make an annual trip to the eye doctor. Doesn't know the smell of optometrist breath, which is always like a strange balance of garlic and Altoids. He doesn't know the feeling of the glaucoma test; sitting in the chair, heart rate accelerating as you prepare for the unpreparable, a little shot of air right on the eyeball. *Alright, for our next test, look through this peephole, and I'm gonna shoot your eye with a Nerf gun.*

But he is three years older and with age comes at least one of three things: you lose some hair, gain a few gray hairs, or experience a decrease in vision. Well, he's still got a full head of non-graying hair, so an attack on the eyes seemed totally reasonable. It happens to everyone.

"Wow, do you have your iPhone set at the 80-year-old display setting?" I asked him like the dirtbag that I am.

"What?" he replied. And it wasn't a defensive 'what,' it was more like "what are you talking about?"

"Your font size. It's out of hand."

"Not at all. See, you gotta give your eyes a break. You're looking at a computer all day, why would you continue to beat them up on the phone?"

This idea immediately fascinated me. I reflected on my experience with eyesight. In fifth grade, I got back the damning result that I needed glasses. At 11 or 12-years-old, that diagnosis feels like a death sentence. *I have to enter middle school on the nerd path?!* Any bully will have one guaranteed "four eyes" bullet to use against me.

So, I fought against it. I rarely wore my glasses in fifth or sixth grade. By seventh grade, my eyes were too bad to continue the resistance. I had no choice but to go full-time glasses. This meant I had the middle school triple threat of glasses, braces, and acne. I grew from 5'2" to 6'2", had no body fat to my name, was just a tall, gangly, voice cracking goon. They say seventh and eighth grade are your prime ugly years and boy do I agree. I fell down the ugly tree and hit every possible branch.

But when I started to wear glasses, it's not as if the lenses healed my eyes. Each year my prescription got a little bit worse.

I now believe the reason for this is because glasses and contacts are admitting defeat. Your eyeballs' morale is depleted by this decision. *Ah, what's the point in trying anymore. He doesn't believe in us.* Each year, the eyes try a little bit less, and things get a little bit worse.

This introduces two Medium Rare alternatives. The first is to do like my brother does. Give your eyes a break when you can. Go with a large font size on your phone. Do the 125 or 150 percent zoom on the computer. When the eyeballs question if they're becoming washed up, you absolutely deny it. *What are you talking about? I don't think this font size looks bigger at all. You two are doing great!* This keeps the morale up and saves your eyes' energy for when you need them most. They're not getting better, but they're probably not getting much worse. The weakness is just that: a weakness.

The other approach is to go full out Army boot camp. Go with the smallest font size possible. Send out emails with 8-pt font and make your co-workers question if you are secretly an alien. Take pleasure in reading the fine print of a legal contract. Never relax. Get five hours of sleep a night. If your eyes aren't veiny and bloodshot, you're not pushing them hard enough.

This second approach seems ridiculous, but if you take this idea outside of eyesight, it is often the recommended approach for how to attack our weaknesses.

Turn your weakness into a strength!

Whatever you hate doing, whatever scares you, do it over and over again until it becomes something you love.

Face your fears and sign up for work league softball!

But why? When did weaknesses have to become strengths? When did we lose the ability to say, "I'm just bad at this particular thing."

What I want to propose, for eyesight and life in general, looks more like the first approach: give your weaknesses a break.

For example, let's say you really want to get better at basketball (you're already pretty good), but you also want to become more assertive because the last time you asked for a raise the conversation ended with you saying, "You know what, I could actually just take a pay cut instead." And you'd also love to learn the guitar (never played before. Always struggled to learn a musical instrument).

The temptation would be to tackle all three at the same time. Become "well-rounded." A true renaissance man or woman. But this strategy forgets two key details. First, there's a limited amount of time in a day. How would you work on all three + have time for a job, relationships, and Netflix? Second, it's far more enjoyable to get closer and closer at mastering one thing than it is to be pretty good (or even just "meh") at several disciplines.

Think about the difference in enjoyment for a basketball player being able to sprint up and down the court for an hour vs. standing over the trash can after one game. Going from standing over the trash can to sprinting up and down the court takes time and dedication. Probably two or three open gyms a week + some regular time spent running on a treadmill.

But it's never a waste of time. That person can compete at a higher level now or go back and play a group of stand-over-the-trash-can opponents and feel like Draymond Green for an hour. Likewise, the person who obsessively practices guitar for four years may not become Jimi Hendrix, but they can feel like Jimi Hendrix whenever they play a beginner's song. The higher you climb in a skill, the more individual levels you've mastered. It's hard work, but there's more fun to be had the further we go into a craft.

Compare that to casually working on a weakness. Let's say you practice the guitar once a week and after three months can do a slow and sloppy rendition of *Smoke on the Water*. I'd argue that's only slightly more enjoyable than not being able to play the guitar at all.

In Robert Greene's book *Mastery*, he details the process of becoming a master in any field. And one of the most important steps is being completely focused on that area, especially at the beginning.

"First, it is essential that you begin with one skill that you can master, and that serves as a foundation for acquiring others. You must avoid at all cost the idea that you can manage learning several skills at a time. You need to develop your powers of concentration and understand that trying to multitask will be the death of the process. Second, the initial stages of learning a skill invariably involves tedium. Yet rather than avoiding this inevitable tedium, you must accept and embrace it."

Learning the right form for shooting a basketball. Learning the chords on a guitar. Seeing someone piling snow on your car and saying to yourself, "You know what, I can be more assertive here." All of these things that eventually come second nature the further we go into developing a skill take a ton of time up front. And, because of the time commitment, because of how tedious these basic skills are to learn, it's tough to spread this type of focused practice out over multiple things.

It's both good and bad news. The good news is, through dedicated hard work, we can push past barriers and catch up to people who had more natural talent than us. Greene uses the example of a famous Air Force pilot named Cesar Rodriguez who found there were people ahead of him (called "the golden boys") who were better, more natural, everything seemed to be easier for them to learn. But he didn't give up. He asked his new instructor to "work him to death." This began an intense training program to turn his weaknesses into strengths.

"He made Rodriguez repeat the same maneuver ten times more than the golden boys, until he was physically sick. He honed in on all of Rodriguez's flying weaknesses and made him practice on the things he hated the most. His criticisms were brutal. One day, however, as he was flying the T-38, Rodriguez had a strange and wonderful sensation—it seemed like he could feel the plane itself at the edge of his fingertips. This is how it must be for the golden boys, he thought, only for him it had taken nearly ten months of intense training."

We can work our weaknesses to death and turn them into strengths. BUT, the bad news, it's not really possible to do this in more than one arena at a time. The chapter on Cesar Rodriguez didn't go on to say he also mastered the guitar and became an NBA All-Star during this same time period.

In the end, I think there are really two defined choices with our weaknesses. We either go all-in, attack them, work extra hard to master or hey, give ourselves a break. Raise the font size. Work on something else instead. With this approach of going all-in or taking it easy, we can get more out of each day and master the things that matter most. Because, at the end of the day, there's a lot more enjoyment going from good to great than from bad to *meh*.

Ideas vs. Execution

"*I'm really more of an idea guy.*"

CHAPTER 24

Dinner for One

Eating alone at a restaurant is a lot harder at dinner than it is earlier in the day.

Anyone worried about eating breakfast alone needs to put that fear aside. The person sitting alone with a newspaper and a stack of pancakes, that person is having the best breakfast. No one else in the restaurant is anywhere close to that level of relaxation. I mean who would you rather be, the parents whose two-year-old just smashed his fist on a plate of scrambled eggs or the lady peacefully filling out the *New York Times* crossword puzzle?

Brunching alone is more challenging. There is a natural coolness to brunch. When I picture brunch, I picture tables with three or four attractive people recapping their amazing night. There are Bloody Marys and Mimosas, and I'm sitting there, alone, with a glass of ice water because I couldn't pull the $4 trigger on freshly squeezed orange juice.

Brunching alone is telling the world, "Well, I didn't have a great night, but I still chose to sleep in 'til 11. And I don't own a waffle iron."

Lunch by yourself is probably the easiest one to pull off. We can bury our faces in the phone, and everyone assumes it's some sort of important work email.

But dinner, whole different story. There's an inherent self-consciousness when you show up to dinner by yourself.

So, I decided to create a list of Medium Rare tips on how to be more comfortable eating dinner alone at a restaurant. These are as much for me as they are for you.

It all starts with owning the situation.

When you enter the restaurant, the host will ask you like Jonah Hill in *Forgetting Sarah Marshall*, "How many tonight?" or the more painful, "Oh, just one?"

Do not let out a sigh. No, "Yeeeeaah, just me." Instead, make it seem like dinner for one is healthy, and anything else would be weird.

So, for example:

Host: Just one?

Response: You bet. Now take me to your finest booth available.

It's not a matter of "what if" you run into someone, you WILL run into someone you know.

I think that's ultimately the biggest fear. What if I'm sitting there and people I know walk in and see me? Won't that be embarrassing?

Because, when you run into someone at a restaurant, every question and answer passes through an "I'm eating dinner alone" filter and automatically sounds depressing.

"How's your job going?"
Answer: Great.
Translation: Can't be too great if you're eating dinner alone.

"How's the family?"
Answer: Great.
Translation: Can't be too great if you're eating dinner alone...

"Oh, how's the French onion soup?"

Answer: It's so good!

Translation: Wow, did you see how excited he was about that bowl of soup? That was really sad to see.

When I go out to eat alone, I go in expecting to run into someone I know. I go on offense. This way, when they do walk through the door, I'm not surprised, and I answer their questions with no defensiveness in my voice and no need to justify why I'm out having dinner alone. There's no shame in taking a selfie with a bowl of French onion soup.

Don't hide in the cell phone

The cell phone can be a nice eating alone crutch. *I'm not eating alone, I'm texting hundreds of my friends right now!*

But try a dinner without it. I'm not advocating for the full-on mindfulness dinner, but something close to it. There is a cool moment midway through dinner without a cell phone when you realize, "Wait, being alone isn't that scary or embarrassing or depressing or whatever else." And once you're enjoying the dinner, even if the people around you are thinking, "Wow, how sad," it doesn't matter. The dinner is still good.

So, go out to dinner. Even if you're alone that night. There is no need to order delivery or reheat leftovers once you've mastered the dinner for one.

In America, forty percent of food is thrown away.
But most of that is cole slaw.

TRASH

Chapter 25

I'm Good with Whatever

"Hey, so what are you thinking for dinner tonight?"

It's a simple question that we never answer with the name of a restaurant. Or even a style of food. Instead, the answer is some variation of this:

"I'm good with whatever."

But it turns out the "whatever" is pretty limited. The conversation usually continues like this:

"I'm good with whatever."

"Alright, how about Italian?"

"Eh, I'm not really feeling Italian."

"Chinese?"

"Eh, I had Chinese for lunch."

"Wait, so what exactly did you mean by 'good with whatever?'"

A couple years ago, I decided I would never say, "I'm good with whatever" again. I started giving concrete answers like: Burger. Pizza. Hot dog.

But that didn't feel right either. Felt like I was making demands. The person would look at me like, "Alright, easy there Putin."

Why is this dinner question so complicated? And why do we pick such a non-committal answer?

One possible answer, to our non-answer, is a concept called "Decision Fatigue." In John Tierney's *New York Times* article, "Do you suffer from decision fatigue?" he frames the problem this way:

"No matter how rational and high-minded you try to be, you can't make decision after decision without paying a biological price. It's different from ordinary physical fatigue — you're not consciously aware of being tired — but you're low on mental energy. The more choices you make throughout the day, the harder each one becomes for your brain, and eventually it looks for shortcuts, usually in either of two very different ways."

The first shortcut, Tierney explains, is to make a bad decision. To not think about the consequences and just go with it because you're tired of weighing things out.

This is why if you propose, "Hey, let's drop a thing of Jameson, mixed with Bailey's, into a glass of Guinness and just chug it," at 11 in the morning, my brain's like, "Are you kidding me? We're gonna do what?"

But fast forward twelve hours later at a bar, I'm absolutely on board. No hesitation.

The other shortcut is to do nothing. Avoid the decision altogether. This is where "I'm good with whatever" lives.

There's another aspect going on here called the "Paradox of Choice." In theory, we think having a bunch of choices is a good thing but, in practice, too many choices freaks us out.

Using that dinner question from earlier, when the choice was, "What do you want for dinner?" that's way too much, too many options available. But think about what happens as it became more specific. Italian? *No.* Chinese? *Nah, had that for lunch.* One way to make decisions easier is to contain the choices to two or three options so we can start weighing out the tangible pros and cons.

We can also defeat "I'm good with whatever" by deciding what we're having for dinner right away in the morning. Our brains haven't been worn down yet by work. At seven in the morning, we go from "I'm good with whatever" to being a creative contestant on Chopped. Open up the fridge: *Ok, I see we've got a half-used thing of ketchup, a couple leftover slices of Digiorno, and a thing of shredded Mexican cheese. Alright, got it! We're going with a strange five-layer lasagna.*

Imagine knowing what was ahead for dinner all day long. You'd have anticipation building from 9 to 5. Even if we're tired after work, the only effort left is firing up the Instant Pot pressure cooker. If you haven't used one of these things yet, you really should. It's like installing a wizard in your kitchen. Throw in a lb of pulled pork in the Instant Pot: great bbq meal an hour later. Same thing with ribs. It can make rice. It can make yogurt. I think in two years, the Instant Pot will be capable of creating human life.

And while the Instant Pot and microwave shine during the work week, the weekend is all about slowing things down with the Crock-Pot. A Saturday or Sunday crockpot, plus some Tupperware, you're set for the week. The Crock-Pot is like the guy at the hotel/resort who you always see sitting in the hot tub; after a few days it's not clear if these are multiple visits or one long stay.

By making the decision to prepare earlier in the day, or plan ahead over the weekend, we can slowly phase out the, "What are you thinking for dinner?" question and it's frustrating, "I'm good with whatever" answer.

I think that's a decision we all can live with.

The Red "Delicious" Apple

CHAPTER 26

I Heard That Was Disappointing

Over 360 billion Oreos have been sold in the last 100 years. The first Oreo was sold on March 6, 1912. And this cookie of a hundred plus years ago was pretty much the same as the Oreos we have today.

"DOUBLE STUF" wasn't introduced until 1974-75; Halloween Oreos (1991) and Christmas Oreos (1995). Nowadays, it seems like a new Oreo flavor is rolled out every other week.

Oreos' friendly competitor on the shelf is the Chips Ahoy! cookie. Chips Ahoy! (a proud supporter of the exclamation point) stormed onto the scene in 1963. The concept was simple - could you mass-produce chocolate chip cookies that would rival homemade versions.

Chips Ahoy! had a ton of confidence from the very beginning. Their early slogans, "You cannot take a bite without hitting a chocolate chip" or "Betcha bite a chip" were taunting their consumers, challenging us to find a better chocolate chip cookie in the store or, dare I say, even go chip-to-chip against Grandma's.

Now, to be fair, nothing will ever beat our mom or grandma's chocolate chip cookies fresh out of the oven, but if a company could even come close to this, mastering the store-bought take on America's favorite cookie, then Oreo would genuinely have some competition on the grocery store shelves.

For years the two cookies have been able to get along, despite the close competition. I think mainly because Oreo was able to say, "Hey, I'm the best at my thing, Chips Ahoy! is the best at its thing." When I grab a thing of Chips Ahoy! you can sense the Oreos saying, *"Hey, good call, tonight feels more like a chocolate chip night."* Likewise, when I grab a thing of Oreos, the Chips Ahoy! shows nothing but support. *"Oooh, you went with the new mint flavor, let me know how that goes!"*

But will this friendliness continue now that revenue numbers are inching closer and closer? Oreos sold $674 million in 2017, Chips Ahoy! wasn't too far behind posting an impressive $619 million. Or how about when Donald Trump was boycotting Oreos as an attack at Nabisco. Chips Ahoy! somehow dodged the President's call-out (which had to create tension in the 1.8 million-square-foot Chicago factory). Or what about in 2014 when Chips Ahoy! rolled out a version with Oreo creme` filling. Oreos had to feel like a line was being crossed. *Dude, we never put chocolate chips on ours. Stay in your lane!*

With all of this crumbling going on in an otherwise stable cookie relationship, I was pleased to find Breyers ice cream playing the role of grocery store peacekeeper. They released a new flavor called the Oreo and Chips Ahoy! 2-in-1. To my knowledge, this is the first time the two have been side-by-side in one ice cream. And, unlike the Chips Ahoy! with Oreo creme`, this one felt like both sides agreed to team up.

So, needless to say, I was extremely excited to give this ice cream a try. Oreo ice cream is already awesome. And chocolate chip cookie dough always gives a strong performance.

Put those two forces together? I was ready to declare this the greatest ice cream ever, even before the first spoonful.

I got to the checkout line, put the ice cream on the belt, watched it slide forward. The cashier scanned the container and then said a shocking but maybe the most effective sentence possible to taper my expectations.

"Oh, I heard that was disappointing."

In sales, every piece of advice is about providing value, communicating value, showing ROI, etc. And so, when I heard this reverse sales pitch, I imagined the look of horror on her manager's face if she overheard this encounter. *I heard that was disappointing?! What were you thinking?!*

But it was exactly what I needed to hear. Before checkout, I was viewing this pint of ice cream as God's gift to mankind. Post-checkout, she brought my expectations back down to earth.

When I prepared a few scoops later that night, I wasn't disappointed at all. Was it great? Not really. I'd say a little bit above average. But since the cashier already took the wind out of my sails, I ended up enjoying the ice cream more than if she had said, "Oh wow, I heard this was amazing!"

I'm now fascinated by this technique. I want to find other ways to pull the 'Oh, I heard this was disappointing' card. Co-worker talks about their upcoming reservation at an amazing new restaurant. "Oh, I heard that place was disappointing." A friend about to go on a two-week vacation. "Oh, I heard Europe is a little disappointing." Family member makes a big decision that they're really proud of? Again, send in the disappointing train to help taper their growing expectations.

Chances are, their event will exceed these new lowered expectations. The person may even take it as a challenge. *Who's he to say this is disappointing? I'll show him. I'll have more fun than I was even planning on.*

And, if the event does fall short, the person can always head to the grocery store, get a thing of milk, choose between Oreos or Chips Ahoy! and know what to expect. Because those two cookies will never disappoint. No matter the expectations.

(research done using the Oreos and Chips Ahoy! Wikipedia pages. And this article on Oreos - https://www.thoughtco.com/history-of-the-oreo-cookie-1779206)

Is there any song more depressing than, "If you're happy and you know it, clap your hands?"

CHAPTER 27

What was the Worst Part of Your Trip?

They walk into the office on a Monday morning. Immediately all of us gather around like a group of villagers welcoming home Odysseus. *He's here! She's here!* We swarm them, wanting a piece of that post-vacation glow. We want to know what life was like on the other side. *Tell us, what was it like over There!*

One by one, the questions flood in.

What was the best part? What'd you do? Where'd you go?

At first, the post-vacation person is happy to oblige. They smile and laugh as they retell various stories. There's a look of nostalgia on their face as they happily bring these memories into the office.

Then comes the first wave of fact-checkers. This group has stayed up to speed with daily alerts. They've followed the person's vacation on Instagram, or Snapchat, or via the GoPro they taped onto the person's suitcase. This round of questions aren't even questions at all, more like statements:

I saw your pictures of Machu Picchu, those were incredible.

Whale watching looked like so much fun.

I bet you had the time of your life in the Uffizi Gallery.

Slowly, the post-vacation glow begins to disappear. In place of that nostalgic look comes one of fatigue. By lunch, you hear the person let out a small sigh when approached with another "How was your trip?" question. By four o'clock, the post-vacation glow has completely faded away. They've snapped. They've grabbed their colleague by the shirt collar, pushed them against the wall. *I said my trip was fine, alright? It was JUST. FINE!*

Now, to be fair, no one is doing anything wrong here. As coworkers, we're all excited and want to hear more. As the post-vacation person, they're doing the best they can to share the energy, they're just hitting the emotional wall of telling the same story over and over again. The stories are becoming played out. It's the same reason we need about four years before we can hear the song *Despacito* again.

The problem is this fatigue begins to chip away at all of the good memories. It goes from, "Man, I wish I could go back" to "I don't want to talk about this trip anymore. I don't want to even *think* about it. I just want to put on my headphones and look at the 200 emails in my inbox."

I want to share a Medium Rare tip that will help your friends and colleagues the Monday after an epic trip. It will sound crazy at first, but it's the best way to help them preserve their sacred memories and even begin to enjoy the bad parts of their vacation. This strategy is a close cousin of, "Oh, I heard that was disappointing."

Here it is: When you see this colleague on a Monday morning, try asking them, "What was the worst part of your trip?"

No one else is asking this question. And the thing is, every trip has bad parts. Layovers. Being on a crowded non-air-conditioned bus. Getting sick from the food. These things happen, but no one feels like they can share these stories for fear of sounding snobby. They fear people will view them as being ungrateful. *Oh, I'm so sorry you had heartburn on your two-week sailing vacation, cry me a fricken river.*

But these bad memories aren't going anywhere. Your friend who saw the Taj Mahal described it as being unforgettable, but equally unforgettable was the night they spent lying on the ground, holding the toilet bowl tight, crying for help after a far too authentic Indian buffet. They will naturally try to bury that memory away.

Unless they get to talk about it.

For example, my buddy Jon visited me and Ashley once in New York City. The trip ended up being pretty bad. Jon was cheap, and I had a lot of big city ego. Big city ego meaning I was used to spending 3x more for things than they should actually be.

On Friday, we went to a restaurant, asked for waters. The waiter opened a $15 bottle of flavored water instead. On Saturday, we walked the entire Brooklyn Bridge followed by the Manhattan Bridge to avoid paying bus/subway fare. Sunday, it was pouring down rain. Jon was rolling his suitcase along the sidewalk. The suitcase somehow caught this lady's foot when we turned the corner. She fell to the ground. A couple blocks later, there was another person just lying down in the middle of the road, legs and arms up like a dead June Bug.

By the time Jon got to the airport, he breathed a sigh of relief. *Get me out of Here.*

But then, I don't know, maybe two weeks later, we started talking about the worst parts of the trip. We laughed about these stories. What was originally a pretty bad trip became almost more fun to reflect on than had it been a great one. The negativity associated with those bad memories had been replaced with humor. The $15 bottle of water. The long walks to avoid paying $2.50 in bus fare. The random June Bug guy. These were now moments of pure comedy.

They say tragedy plus time equals comedy. And that's the beauty of the "What was the worst part of your trip" question. Not only does it help your friend preserve the good memories, it helps them transform bad memories into funny ones. Once your colleague gets started, they will want to share multiple stories.

Oh! And this other time, oh yeah, this part really sucked. You gotta hear this.

Creative kid in a geography class

Question: Name these two countries

Answer:

Chapter 28

Guilt is Good

A week ago, we had a big snow in Chicago. The kind of snow where you bring out the winter boots and spend an unhealthy amount of time thinking you'll get into cross country skiing.

As expected, our car was absolutely covered. Every car on the street needed to be shoveled out.

But there was one car that got singled out like it was the smallest kid on the playground. I don't know why—maybe their car alarm was going off all night—but someone had shoveled a foot of snow on top of this vehicle. The car looked like the guy at the beach who lets his friends bury him in the sand.

I wonder what that person thought when they came back to their car. At what point do you just say, "Welp, I guess I don't have a car anymore."

Or what if the owner looked like Betty White and had the heart of Mr. Rogers? She just got out of choir practice at the Catholic church and saw her car under an avalanche. Imagine the happiness draining away from her face as she begins pushing off the snow with her trembling gloveless hands. She uses her hand-knit Michigan State University scarf as a makeshift shovel.

My hope is whoever piled on the snow felt a little twist of guilt later on that day. They're refilling the coffee pot at work, scooping the grounds, and immediately have a flashback to the shoveling incident. They see a motivational poster in the office that reads something like, *"Character is who you are when nobody's watching."* By lunch, they're like the main character in *The Tell-Tale Heart*; they can't take it anymore. They leave work, grab the shovel, begin digging out the car.

In those moments, we need guilt to kick in. Guilt is the glue that holds society together.

For example, I had a friend who went to the dry cleaners. She paid in change, but on the drive home noticed there was a dime on her seat. She turned the car around and went right back. She gave the dime to a confused worker behind the front desk.

Now, you may hear this story and think eh, that's a little bit extreme. But I hear it and think, "Yes! That's *exactly* the level of guilt our society needs!" Why? Because we know this person will never rob a bank. Or shovel piles of snow onto a car. Or throw someone else's laundry out of a community machine.

I can identify with this type of guilt. One time I flipped someone off in New York City and that night I worried that the person was having such a bad day, maybe the middle finger pushed them over the edge; sent them into a deep depression. And how would I ever know? It wasn't like I could ask around the small town of New York City, *"Hey, do you know if that one guy is doing ok?"*

The list continues on. I've always been too afraid to tell a "yo mama joke" for fear the response would be, "Dude, his mom died last week." I use the word "frick" just to avoid the Midwestern f-bomb guilt. And one year, right before March Madness, I convinced myself that all my trash talk to a friend about Tom Izzo and Michigan State would come back to bite me when the Jayhawks played the Spartans (thankfully, the Jayhawks won, but I haven't said a negative word since).

As nice guys, we get way too much credit. Kindness is often the prettier, better-marketed version of guilt. It's like how the poncho is just a well-marketed garbage bag. A lot of times the reason "nice" people stay away from being mean is we don't want to go home and enter that brass-knuckled boxing match with guilt.

The problem is our guilt isn't always rewarded. I worked in telephone customer service for about two years after college. One of my friends got yelled at on the phone. We all got yelled at. We almost looked forward to it because the bad calls became the best comedy.

But, after this particular incident, and I mean two or three months later, the guy called back, asked to be transferred to her. Then he apologized. He said he was going through some stuff at the time and felt really bad for how he treated her over the phone. My friend was shocked. We were all shocked.

But we didn't give him a discount...

Too often, the customers that put up the biggest fuss end up getting 10 percent off, or a full refund, or NFL Sunday Ticket free for the next 15 seasons. In contrast, the customers who have too much guilt to put up a fuss will pay the full price. I feel like guilt even gets punished.

You waited how long on hold? And you're not demanding a discount? Here, you coward, I'm gonna go ahead and charge you 10 percent more. Maybe you can grow a spine next time and complain about it! You don't even have the guts to speak to my manager, do you? Do you!

Or look at politics. In theory, we'd want politicians who were honest and could own up to making a mistake. But what tends to happen—on either side of the aisle—is any time a politician says "I'm wrong" or "I'm sorry," the pitchforks come out. *Get 'em! Get that lousy flip flopper!* A week later their political career is over.

I think we need to start rewarding guilt. If you buy a song on iTunes, you should get an email every month that says, "Hey, we noticed you'd feel too guilty downloading these songs for free somewhere else. Here's some store credit." When the words "sorry" or "thank you" are said to a customer service rep, an immediate 10 percent discount should be applied. When you bring a dime back to the dry cleaners, hey, the next shirt is on us.

If there are no incentives to have guilt, kindness starts to erode away. We need the balance. For every shoveler piling snow onto a car, we need the guy in the Kansas Jayhawks sweatshirt watching from the office window. He notices the lady has a Michigan State scarf. He tries not to look at the motivational poster.

Ah, I should really go dig them out. Wouldn't want to lose the basketball game...

Character is who you are when nobody's watching.

Man quietly farts in the back of an Uber. Driver quietly gives him a 1-star review.

CHAPTER 29

Sometimes You Hop in The Car with a Stranger

Sometimes you have to break up with your dentist. Not because of anything they did or didn't do, but because your health plan changes and, naturally, well, you just kind of drift apart.

It's a situation that shouldn't be stressful at all, but since I am the king of turning the simple into sizzles, I handled this situation about as awkwardly as humanly possible.

Awkward meaning I called the lady at the front desk to end things and five minutes later called what I thought was a different office to schedule an appointment. I heard her typing on the keyboard. A little bit of silence. "Mr. O'Brien, didn't you just cancel with us?"

I was in need of a new dentist, but more importantly, on that late December night, I was in need of a Tenderizer sandwich.

The Tenderizer may be the best sandwich in all of Chicago. Or at least the best sandwich in Chicago after midnight. Think grilled cheese sandwich on Texas toast but with chicken tenders, bacon, hot sauce, bbq sauce, dip it in some ranch. Oh babay! It is the quintessential late-night meal. It's just as good as Chick Fil A or the infamous

Popeyes chicken sandwich. The restaurant/bar is called Cheesies, which was kind of walking distance from my old apartment.

But not walking distance in the winter. I looked down the street and saw the bus two stoplights ahead. I checked my phone for the next arrival. 19 minutes. It was now or never, and I really wanted the Tenderizer.

Sometimes you break into a dead sprint for the first time in months to catch the Cheesies Express Bus. My lungs immediately shouted, *"Retreat! Retreat!"* but I kept pushing. I had the voice of my high school strength and conditioning coach in my head, *"The pain of regret is going to be worse than the pain you're feeling right now. Dig deeper! Go, go, go!"*

I caught up to the back of the bus. I put my hand in the air. *Wait!* The light turned green and the bus was back in drive. I was so, so very close. I stopped at the edge of the curb, hands on top of my head, trying to catch my breath. It was over. Time to turn around and head home. Go to sleep on an empty stomach.

As I stood there in defeat, catching my breath, a black Lincoln pulled up to the curb. The passenger side window rolled down.

"Need a ride?"

First instinct, of course, was to say no. Years of "stranger-danger" talks in elementary school prepare you for this exact moment.

But... the Tenderizer. It's just. So. Good.

I looked in and the driver seemed like she was about 60-65 years old. The man in the passenger seat looked to be around the same age. Seemed safe enough. I walked to the back door. And, just to be clear, this was pre-Uber. I was genuinely embarking on some uncharted hop-in-a-car-with-a-stranger territory.

As I reached out for the door handle, the strength and conditioning coach was replaced with my mom and my wife's voice, *"Are you kidding me?! Chris, turn around right now!"*

Too late. Door closed. I was either going to Cheesies or going to be a future storyline on Law & Order.

Sometimes you scan the backseat for any red flags. Blindfolds. Hatchets. Chainsaws. I found nothing. Just a People magazine on the floor, which that's about as innocent as it gets. The radio was on a religious station. They asked me about what I did for a living, kept the car at a comfortable 73 degrees. This was the very definition of a pleasant car ride. There was nothing strange about these strangers.

But I still kept waiting for the plot twist. When were they going to pull off these incredibly realistic looking masks? When do I get thrown in the trunk? When do they toss me in Lake Michigan?

We pulled up to Cheesies and I thanked them for the ride. I wasn't sure if I needed to pull out cash for a tip. And then came a twist that I know will sound made up for the sake of the story, but I promise you it's 100 percent real.

"Hey, are you looking for a dentist by chance?" the driver said.

Seriously...

"Actually, I kind of am," I replied.

"Well," the driver said. She gestured to the man in the passenger seat. "His office is right over there. Here, let me give you a business card."

Dinner and a dentist. Two problems solved in one car ride. That's why sometimes in life you hop in the car with a stranger.

Hailing a cab is a great way to tell your date, "Hey, I still carry a flip phone."

CHAPTER 30

Moral Dilemma in the Laundry Room

On a Sunday night, open laundry machines go faster than Hamilton tickets. It's not at all like a Friday night when every machine is wide open, dancing around the laundry room singing, "Be our guest! Be our guest!"

On a Sunday night, you wait. And wait. And wait some more.

One of the tough parts about community laundry is just because the timer on the washing machine or dryer displays zero doesn't guarantee it's opening any time soon. The person might show up an hour later.

It's at this point when I'm left with the hardest moral dilemma anyone can face in a community laundry room. Do I remove the clothes from the dryer? Do I put the pile of dry clothes in a big blob on the table nearby and keep the assembly line moving? Or do I just sit there for the rest of the evening waiting, politely, before giving up and saying, "Welp, better luck next week."

It's a hard call to make because I've been the victim of a laundry piler before. I had occupied two machines, went upstairs, and fell asleep during an NFL game. An hour or so later, I came back downstairs and caught the laundry piler red-handed. She had my clothes in her hands, dropping things on the floor as she went to toss them on a table. She wasn't sorting, she was shoveling.

A lot goes through your head in that moment. The first is complete shock. *Wait, the Laundry Piler is an actual person?* Up until then, I just imagined the Tasmanian Devil coming in, laughing hysterically, throwing clothes at random out of the machines.

The second emotion is righteous anger. You feel like you're the police breaking up a crime. Right as I was ready to channel my best cop voice and shout, "Freeze - put the laundry down!" the last wave of emotion rushed in, and this one was far less confident.

"Hey," I said softly, like a little kid catching their parents stealing their Halloween candy. "Those are mine."

"Yeah, well," the lady replied. She shrugged and put the last handful of my clothes onto the pile. She proceeded to put her laundry in the machines.

Flooded with these hot-blooded laundry room flashbacks, I stood there, mano a mano with the drying machine, antsy, impatient and wrestling with my past laundry room trauma. In that bare-naked moment of truth, I was tortured with one question and one question only: Do I have what it takes to sink down to the lowest possible form of laundry etiquette and become a laundry piler myself?

I looked at the dryer again, then looked at the chaotic scene around me. On a Friday night, you wait. You give the person the benefit of the doubt. But on a Sunday night, all order has been thrown out the window. Sunday nights are filled with chaos, anarchy, and an anything-goes attitude.

Right at this moment, a woman rushed down the stairs with an empty laundry basket. She went to the dryer, apologized, and started grabbing her clothes. "I'm sorry. I lost track of time."

She went over to the washing machine, and I thought oh no, this is a classic Sunday night move. She's going to put her freshly washed clothes in the dryers she just used. I've seen this move before.

It's based on a shaky ideology called "The Territory Rule," which states once you put your clothes in a machine, that becomes YOUR machine for the rest of the night. The laundry machines become like parking spaces. I'm getting ready to fight this, but I can't. It's Sunday night laundry. Anything goes.

"Alright," she says. "Sorry for making you wait. Dryers are all yours."

And I'm sure the nice/guilty thing to say would have been oh no, no, you can finish up, that's ok, but I'll leave the politeness for a Friday night. I started loading my clothes in the dryers and she made her way to one of the waiting seats. I looked around at the other dryers, two minutes left, one-minute left, one was at zero. As I went to the stairs, I knew her own moral dilemma was underway. My guess is she would be like me, not willing to become the laundry piler, but secretly wishing the Tasmanian Devil would storm in and bring some sense of order to the Sunday night chaos.

Spinal Surgery

Guy 1: I heard your spine surgery was really expensive.
Guy 2: Yeah, but not having one was costing me a lot more.

CHAPTER 31

Celebrate BEFORE the Signature

Don't celebrate until it's official. Until the ink has dried on the signature. Until the money has deposited into your bank account.

There are so many phrases, so many pieces of advice that belabor this point not to celebrate too early. This has become so ingrained in us that we start acting really weird when good news is right around the corner. We start saying things like "don't jinx it" or "knock on wood." We become extra humble as if our fate—like a prison sentence—hinges on our good behavior. If we even *think* about pumping our fist in an early celebration, we see a nun at the chalkboard reminding us: Pride goeth before the fall.

For 29 years, I've accepted this superstition, never once asking why this is our established norm. But a couple of weeks ago, right as I was daring to celebrate a little too early, and thus getting ready to correct myself with some sort of "Well, it's not official yet" statement, I thought, "You know what, no, I'm going to keep on celebrating."

Because think about the reverse. Think about how many times we let ourselves experience negative emotions for the things that haven't—and may never—actually happen. We imagine the plane crashing. The presentation going horribly. Our loved ones getting into an accident. We allow ourselves to experience all of these preemptive strikes of anxiety all in the name of good old-fashioned worry.

I mean really, when it comes right down to it, worry, anxiety, and fear are like "celebrating" bad news before it's official.

But heaven forbid you try it the other way around; letting yourself feel all of the good stuff too soon.

My dad made a good point about why this sentiment has stuck with us. He thinks part of it is because we're so used to movies where they show a happy group of people hopping into a car, they're singing, dancing, and as an audience, you know that yep, this is when the semi-truck blindsides them.

Or the main character is having the best day ever, just got a promotion at work, which of course means the phone call later that night will be news that their mom or dad passed away.

Go ahead and re-watch *Remember the Titans*. That movie is the best example I've ever seen of bad news immediately following the happiest moments. There's always a valley right after the peak. It's only fitting the team literally sings, "Aint no mountain high, aint no valley low" in the locker room.

Our standard operating procedure is to experience the bad stuff before it happens and then wait, hope, cross our fingers for any of the good stuff.

But here for a second, let's imagine a different approach. Imagine a scenario where you celebrate each step of the way. If it's a money thing, daydream about what you'll do with the upcoming cash infusion. Maybe buy a couple things on credit before the money has deposited. If it's a new job, start writing drafts of your triumphant LinkedIn announcement even before the interview. If it's a new house, drink the biggest margarita of your life the night you put in an offer. Don't let the "yeah, but we could still lose" part of the brain spoil all of the fun.

Then, even if the good thing falls apart right at the last second, you were still able to have multiple celebrations along the way. You had weeks/months of pure preemptive happiness. And, in the end, yeah it sucks things didn't pan out, but we're not beating ourselves up over stepping on a sidewalk crack, not knocking on wood, or whatever other walking on eggshells excuse can pop up in the "don't celebrate too early" mindset.

"Celebrate before the signature" is really just another way of saying "having hope" or "having faith." Faith and hope are the perfect antidotes to worry. In the words of Hebrews 11, "Faith is the confidence that what we hope for will actually happen; it gives us assurance about things we cannot see." When looking at the future, we'll never know with 100 percent certainty what's going to happen, and this is where worry, fear, and anxiety like to check into the hotel room for a couple of nights and play a heated game of kickball right in the stomach. To fight those emotions off, why not start celebrating a little bit early, hoping for the best rather than planning for the worst.

If we continue to live in the original mindset, we also risk our signature moment being a little bit of a letdown. We put the "official" moment way too high on a pedestal. *I waited all this time to experience this? I'm not even that happy!*

It's also a risky move to wait for the "official" moment because you're banking on this day being perfect in every other area of life. But way too often you get the bonus check on the same day your car needs a $2,000 repair. You get the new job just in time to find out a year's worth of electric bills didn't go through. You lay down on the couch, let out a nice big relaxed sigh, only to hear, "Chris, he has to go out."

In this new Medium Rare approach, one where you "celebrate before the signature," it should look like the person who is booking a really nice dinner reservation. There's a celebration every step of the way. They've got the moment of celebration when they book the time over the phone. The mini-celebrations when people ask about their dinner plans, and they confidently say, "I'm going Here" and people ooh and ahh. *I'd love to go There.* The celebration of getting dressed up, splurging for the regular Uber vs. an Uber Pool. The wine, the appetizers, the main course. The dessert that the waiter lights on fire. The Monday back at work talking about the dinner, answering the, "How was it?" questions still on a championship high.

When you celebrate before the signature, it's hard to tell where the climax is because everything leading up to the event and everything afterward keeps the party going.

So, celebrate when it's unofficial. Before the ink has dried on the signature. Before the money has deposited into your bank account. Worst case scenario: it ends up being a letdown. But I think it's better to come down than to never be looking up.

Man lands dream job at the top of the Sears Tower. Realizes on Day 1 that he's afraid of heights.

Chapter 32

What's Your Name Again?

Have you ever been at a party and someone walks up to you, introduces themselves, then literally like one nanosecond after they say their name, poof, it's already gone? For the rest of the night (maybe for the next five years) you'll greet them as, "Hey man!" or "Hey buddy, what's going on?"

This scenario has happened to all of us; which makes me wonder, how many times has it happened in reverse. Where I'm the nameless one. The, "Man" in "Hey man!"

It's hard to grasp because it's hard to picture ourselves not at the center of the universe. And not in a full-out narcissistic way; it's just human nature. Even the humblest person views themselves as the main character in their specific story (albeit an incredibly humble, selfless hero).

Even if you're like, "Maybe I *used to* view things that way, but not anymore. I'm living for my kids," or "It's all about my grandkids," in those scenarios you are still the Academy Award-winning Best Supporting Actor. You're the Alan Arkin or the Octavia Spencer. The movie is not the same without you.

My point is this, no one's walking down the sidewalk thinking, "You know what, I'm just an unpaid extra here. The movie is really about that stranger across the street."

But in their movie, that's exactly who I am. I'm the unpaid extra!

And, because we see ourselves as the main character, every decision we make is framed through this all-important protagonist lens. Which college to go to. Which job to take. Should I throw that person's laundry out of the machine? These become significant moments in the plot line of our story. "The Hero's Journey." So, as we make these decisions, it becomes this mixture of what do I want to do (how should I write this story) and also what will other people think of my choice (the audience's reaction).

But the truth is, outside of our immediate family, maybe a couple of close friends and a few co-workers, all of these moments really aren't a big deal for anyone else.

How do I know? Because think about what it's like when someone who you haven't seen since high school posts on Facebook that they got engaged. You go, "Oh wow, that's great, I remember they sat next to me in math class." And then they're gone from our brain because we're worried about the deadline at work, or your kids at school, or a million other little things. Then, three years later, we see a photo of this person holding a baby. Same mental cycle. "Oh wow, good for them. I remember they sat next to me in math class." Give it a Like. Keep scrolling.

The same thing is happening in reverse. If Ashley puts up wedding photos, vacation photos, or I share a Medium Rare blog post, a distant acquaintance sees this and thinks, "Oh, neat, good for them. I remember the time he farted next to me in math class." Give it a Like. Keep scrolling.

The truth is, we are not at the center of everyone else's universe. This goes for famous people too. Case and point, I was listening to a podcast hosted by JJ Redick, a famous basketball player from Duke who has been playing in the NBA for 10+ years. He was talking about how hard free agency was for him and how long it took to find a team that would give him an appealing offer. He said he was embarrassed about it all. He didn't want to go out in public because he thought he'd just feel all the shame, everyone would be looking at him, whispering about him, viewing him as a loser.

What he found was that no one (outside of his family and close friends) was thinking about him or his free agency situation. People were thinking about their own lives. Their family, their friends, their own big decisions. When friends and acquaintances talked to him, they were simply happy to see him. *"Hey JJ, what's going on!"* And, to most people, his situation was still one to be envied. NBA player. Making millions of dollars. That's every kid's dream.

But if he were to open up and say, "Hey, I'm going through a hard time right now" the reality is people wouldn't look down on him or cheer on his misfortune (unless they're a North Carolina Tar Heels fan). Most people would be there to help and show empathy.

This creates an interesting contrast, the moments when we feel the most alone and don't want to share what's going on are actually the moments when people would care the most. For instance, look at all of the "thoughts and prayers" messages people receive after a death in the family.

And the same thing with good news. Hundreds of likes for an engagement ring or a picture of a newborn baby. When we see someone else's victory, we pretty much always celebrate along with them.

But it's all the stuff in the middle, those regular everyday decisions, the minor setbacks, the minor disappointments; these things really matter to us but it's not a big deal to anyone else. There are no CNN panels breaking down the daily action in our lives.

It introduces a weird truth: people are generally cheering for each other in the good times, helping each other in the bad times, and all the little stuff in between they're thinking about their own lives instead. Which means a lot of our life flies under the radar.

Realistically, there are only like eight people in the world who can say they are the main characters in more than their immediate circle's lives. I'd say the list is limited to Trump, Kanye, Kim Kardashian,

Beyonce, LeBron, Elon Musk, Michelle Obama, and Lady Gaga. For the rest of us, our big decisions don't make it to the top of the headlines.

Now, I feel like this chapter is a giant balancing act. It gets back to the Ernie Banks at a pizza place philosophy, and I can understand how this could all read in a depressing, "What's the point? We don't matter," type of way.

But I don't think it's depressing at all. I think it's the opposite. I think if we fully appreciate we're only a main character, only a main supporting character, in a small group of family and friends' lives, it allows us to hyper-focus our time on the people who matter most to us, focusing on the plot points in that story and not wasting our time overthinking our perceived impact everywhere else. We can make decisions that are best for us and those it directly impacts. It's a far more reasonable, more relaxing way to live.

Because, the truth is, if you put a microphone in someone's brain as we walked by, they're not standing there reviewing our last year of successes and failures. Their thoughts probably sound more like this:

"What's your name again?"

Deleting Facebook is a great way to find out who actually knows when your birthday is

CHAPTER 33

Big Decisions are Overrated

Life is full of big decisions. But they don't really start until age 17.

Prior to 17, most of life's big decisions—i.e., where you'll live, which sports teams to support, which school to go to—are decided by your parents. There is also a giant head-start shaping our views on religion, politics, and whether or not LeBron James is better than Michael Jordan.

I'd say maybe the only "big decision" areas, pre-17, were choices on drugs, sex, and alcohol.

And then bam, just like that, you go from no big decisions at all to having the (seemingly) biggest decision of your life. College. Where to go. To go at all. Your choice here, as we were told, will determine everything. Your career. Your earning potential. Your chance to ever be happy again.

Late spring of my senior year, as close to the final deadline as possible, I narrowed my choices down to two radically different options. Hope College (small, Christian, Liberal Arts college three hours away from home) vs. Kansas University (huge, 14 hours away, but it would be close to my grandparents). At Hope, I was "hoping" (pun intended) to keep playing basketball. At Kansas, I was going to watch my favorite basketball team, in person, at the historic Allen Fieldhouse.

I made a pros/cons list, and the only thing my list achieved was making the decision feel even more complicated. It was so much of a win-win decision that it morphed into a lose-lose.

I chose Hope and by January of my Freshmen year, it looked like I had made a terrible mistake. I was miserable. Sad. Pathetic. I almost exclusively wore a pair of gray Kansas Jayhawks sweatpants (not that there's anything wrong with that!) and any footage of me from that era was in black and white with sad jazz music playing in the background.

I was ready to leave. Filled out a transfer form to KU. Filled out a transfer form to Central Michigan University. I was very much in the "anywhere but Hope" camp.

Then, just a year later, Hope was the greatest place in the world. Two years after that, I was wearing a cap and gown sitting in the Devos Fieldhouse, on a basketball court I never played on, with my girlfriend/future wife several rows ahead. We were all listening to the commencement speaker, Heather Sellers, who was one of my favorite English professors; a teacher who secured what I had known (and at times forgotten) since first grade: I want to be a writer.

I think it can be tempting to summarize this whole Hope vs. Kansas story as, "See, that's why you gotta stick with things, be persistent, never quit. Look how it all turned around." But I think there was a more subtle lesson being taught. The subtle lesson was finding out just how little my initial "big college decision" actually mattered in the end.

Here's what I mean: I think I would have hit the same internal/external challenges at Kansas as I did at Hope during my freshman year. Those challenges being: new environment, starting over, being away from home. The college choice was kind of like choosing between pasta and buffalo wings with the goal of not getting heartburn; either way, it was going to happen.

And I would have had the same turnaround story at KU as I did at Hope. It's very possible that either choice (Hope or Kansas) would have worked out just fine. The initial "big" decision really didn't matter as much as the small everyday choices afterward.

When I dig into what made things turn around, I realize the formula was pretty simple. The biggest thing was building a community. I went from having a great group of friends in high school to a great new group of friends in college. This took time to build. High school friends you've known for four, five, ten plus years. College friends you've known for, what, five weeks?

Then I started dating Ashley. We went to New York City together for our second semester junior year; part of a "study abroad" program. Does New York City count as a foreign country? Compared to Holland, Michigan, absolutely. Might even be a different planet.

There we were, together, fourteen hours away. No trips home. Nine million strangers around us. Mice running around the apartment. Giant rats in the subway. Ninety-nine cent slices of pizza dripping with more grease than sauce. It was a sloppy chaotic paradise, and I loved every second of it.

But could I have done it at 18-years-old, fresh out of high school?

Probably not. But maybe. It may have just been harder. May have been more homesick. May have worn sweatpants more often. Either way, things in NYC working out or failing, it's because of the small everyday choices, not the big initial decision to hop on a plane.

The problem with putting too much weight on big decisions is it implies that everything after is static; that our list of priorities will be in the same exact order the moment we make the decision as it will be a year, five years, ten years later. That what we care about today will always be what we care about tomorrow.

But the reality is, all of these big decisions impact our current self and our future self. And that future self, just like our current self, is a mix of our Best Self, our Worst Self, and our "Meh" Self.

What's the Meh Self? It's the random Tuesday in October self that just wants to auto-pilot the day, get home, maybe do some Friday night laundry.

And the Worst Self isn't thinking about how great things are. It's thinking about how much the commute sucks, how cold it is outside, how the car alarm won't stop beeping.

It'd be great if Best Self was always at the wheel—the one that always thinks positive, picks the salad over a Big Mac, sees nothing but good in the people around them—but it's not practical. Life is a mixture of all three; the Good, the Bad, and the Meh. And if the Bad and the Meh are winning the majority of the time, then any decision, any situation—no matter how good—will ultimately start to suck.

Bad and Meh Self will find a way to complain that Hawaii is too hot. That the wine in Napa Valley is too expensive. That their knees hurt in the Ufizzi Gallery. On the flip-side, Best Self can lose heat in December and still say, "Isn't it great to have the whole family cuddled together under this one blanket? I love a good Midwestern winter. What do ya say we go to a Cleveland Browns game?"

I came to the conclusion that "big decisions are overrated," and this philosophy served as my guiding light in all of the big decisions that came up after college. I thought I had this all figured out until March of 2018. A big decision came along that hit me harder than Thanos in the final *Avengers* movies.

In March of 2018, I worked harder than ever on all of my different ideas and writing projects. Before work, after work. Saturdays. Sundays. It consumed me. I made Captain Ahab, Michael Jordan, and Wile E. Coyote look like the ideal models for work-life balance. I wanted to prove to myself that I could do it; justify that if I quit my job, I could keep up at my current pace, plus add 40 more hours Monday through Friday.

How did this fit into our marriage? My wife is incredibly supportive, but she does it in a rational way. She's less of the cheerleading, *"Chris, Chris, he's our man, if he can't do it, no one can!"* and more tactical; more alright, well if this is the decision, then this is what comes next. When I said I was thinking about quitting my job, going all-in on these ideas, she said, "Ok, but that means we will sell the condo, likely move in with parents."

In that moment, I was like, "I mean, I want my dream, but let's not get *too* carried away here."

One night, right in the thick of this go-go-go pursuit, she had me write out a list. Ten words to describe who I am. I wrote things like: idea guy, writer, entrepreneur, dreamer. I read them off.

Ashley replied, "So, nothing like son, grandson, uncle, friend?"

Oof. Thankfully I put husband on the list!

My first reaction was that this was a trick question. I didn't know I was supposed to list off who I was in terms of relationships. But then it clicked, it wasn't a trick at all. My list was painfully accurate. I truly wasn't thinking about anything other than my projects.

The big decision of staying or leaving my job had boiled down to which will make me "more creatively fulfilled." Which has more writing. Which is more in line with "following the dream."

But the thing is, there are way more factors at play in that type of decision. There's my marriage, family, relationships, house payments, potential for starting a family without being too deep in debt, or even continuing to live in the expensive city of Chicago. Continuing to live on our own.

And those are just the major factors. There are also the micro ones too; the little luxuries in life like being able to spend $10 ordering a Tenderizer vs. slumming it up with the Filet-O-Fish handout at a Catholic Church.

And that's where the internet delivers its counter punch. You'll see things like this:

If you can't handle the suffering, you clearly don't want your dream bad enough.

Insert long list of billionaires who talk fondly about those lean years and having negative balances in their bank accounts. Massive credit card balances. Was it worth it? Yep. Now I have ten billion reasons why I'm glad I never gave up. When the going gets tough, the tough get going.

Hey, good for them. But notice none of those videos were recorded during the actual sucky part. And no videos exist talking about the people who didn't find the billion-dollar pot of gold at the end of the struggling rainbow. We don't see all of the restaurants and start-ups shutting their doors.

So, I started to do my own guerrilla research. I reached out to people via LinkedIn, reached out to colleagues who I knew worked on writing projects on the side, or side businesses. I basically just started cold calling people and asked for advice.

One of the people I talked to said things changed for him when he realized both the art, and the day job, neither one was his sole identity. He was also a husband and a dad. When he thought about what "making it" looked like, he realized there would still be things to complain about as a full-time writer. There'd be editor notes. Negative reviews. Shows being canceled. There's always room for "Worst Self" and "Meh Self" to weasel their way back into the equation.

And that's when the light bulb went on for me. I thought back to the Hope vs. Kansas decision and remembered that what turned things around were the relationships, not any sort of personal success or "following my dreams" fulfillment. It was more important to have great people to share things with than having great things to share.

I was reminded of this last week at the grocery store. They have an escalator where you can put your shopping cart and the escalator carries it up to the second floor. I was coming down the opposite escalator and saw a completely empty shopping cart except for one thing of guacamole. I looked at it and started laughing. When I came home, I shared the story with Ashley.

"Who gets one thing of guacamole, decides 'Yeah, I can't carry this AND ride an escalator at the same time. That's way too much pressure. Especially with the Escalator Dictator behind me breathing down my neck.'"

This seems crazy to say, but I was happier sharing a story about a container of guacamole riding an escalator than I was at my creative "peaks" back in March when the projects were all that mattered and I was running on low sleep, low family time, low relationships. The same thing happened the next day when I saw a guy driving in a BMW convertible, texting at a stoplight, blaring the song "Jump Around" at 8:15 in the morning. Again, I started laughing. I wanted to share the story with my wife, my friends, my co-workers and, eventually, share it here in the book.

Writing, in its purest form, is really just an extension of community. You're sharing stories with friends; some of whom you'll never actually meet.

In the end, happiness isn't all that complicated. It isn't an accomplishment, a dollar amount, or one big final milestone. Happiness is watching a thing of guacamole ride an escalator. Or dumping a full tray of ice cubes into a Master Cup. Or a Saturday morning, when you're writing the final paragraph to a book that may or may not sell many copies, in a condo that you and your wife may or may not be able to afford, with a dog who you love (at least 92 percent of the time) nestled right under your arm.

In that moment, the Best Self, Worst Self, and Meh Self are all in agreement — you know what, things worked out pretty well. It's good to be Here.

And as that feeling starts to settle in, I can't help but look ahead at the next year, the next five years, the next ten years and begin to wonder, *"Hey, what's going on over There?"*

I feel like guacamole raises its price by 25 cents each week just to see if we'll ever notice

Acknowledgements

Writing a book is far from a solo endeavor. I have a ton of thank yous to share to the people who empowered this book to go from rough draft to physical book. I'll go in chronological order.

First, thank you to ChicagoNow for hosting my Medium Rare blog. Every one of these chapters started out as a blog post.

Once the rough draft was complete, it was time to send it out to my Supreme Court of Editors: Michele Popadich, Omar Muniz, Lynn Zukerman, David Daskal, Lainey Tick, Pam Kala, Jon Oldham, and my Mom and Dad. The rough draft they received had 57,000 words and 36 chapters. After their notes and feedback, the final draft ended up at 42,000 words and 33 chapters. That last review step—sending your book off to incredibly smart, helpful readers/editors—is so important to the overall process. I'm lucky to have this group!

With the editing complete, now it was time to make some cartoons. The amazing artwork was created by KG. You should have seen the sloppy stick figure drawings I sent over originally with notes like, "I'm thinking something like this." KG truly created something out of nothing. These cartoons are as important as the written chapters. It wouldn't be the same book without them.

Now it's time for the cover design. The artwork and design was created by Bruno Rodriguez. Bruno does an outstanding job distilling the themes of the book into one image. I'm hoping to work with him on every book cover for the rest of my writing career!

Thank you to both Mark Rader and my Dad for reviewing the back of the book description, lending their expert marketing perspectives. And thank you to Psalmyy on Fiverr for all of his hard work (and patience) formatting the text into a physical book.

And last but certainly not least, thank you to my wife, Ashley, for being my rock. Writing a book can be an incredibly long and often discouraging process. I couldn't have made it to the finish line without your steady encouragement. I love you with all my heart.

About Long Overdue Books + Upcoming Projects

There is a book called *From the Place of Gathering Light* by Kathleen Stocking. It's the best book I've read in 20 years. But you won't find it on Amazon. It's hard to locate in a Google search. However, if you travel up to northern Michigan, to the local independent bookstores in Traverse City, Northport, Sutton's Bay, you'll see it everywhere. Back in the summer of 2019, I walked into Horizon Books in downtown Traverse City and there was a giant poster of the cover. Multiple copies of the book.

Online, Kathleen Stocking flies under the radar. Up North, she's a rockstar.

The whole experience got me thinking: Maybe books don't have to end up on Amazon. Maybe the better home for books is the local bookstores where life slows down for a second and we're not constantly checking our phones.

My long-term goal is to turn Long Overdue Books into two physical brick and mortar bookstores. One would be in Chicago, the other on Old Mission Peninsula in Traverse City. Until then, maybe I'll build a Little Free Library location. And try to capture the feeling of a local bookstore on our website. I want it to be a place where everyone's invited and readers can always discover new authors.

On the website, authors have the chance to submit their work in the "Seeking Editor" or "Seeking Publisher" categories. Instead of sending their manuscript off to literary agents, authors can simultaneously build and connect with an audience while working to improve their book, eventually get a final copy out there. I'll also have a section on the site called, "Please, Take These Ideas" where I'll post a mock cover design and a general idea for a book/movie/TV show that's totally free for the taking. First come, first serve. This is my way of helping any writer who says, "I'd love to write a book, but I just haven't had an idea yet." I don't want that to be a barrier.

The finished books on the site, like *Here or There*, won't be shipped in 24 hours. No delivery drones either. We'll do one shipment a month for all orders. Eventually I picture these orders coming in a box (similar to like Blue Apron or Barkbox) where you'd receive the copy of the book, a few items that relate to the book, and a letter from the author about how the idea came about.

No clicks. No likes. No number of pageviews. I don't want Long Overdue Books to feel like social media. And reviews aren't going to be a 5-star system like Amazon or your last Uber ride. Readers can send in their reviews, thoughts, feedback to library@longoverduestories.com and we'll get it over to the author. Why not build a better connection between readers and writers? Build a community out of this, just like the local bookstore.

A Publishing Experiment

Depending on when you are reading this book, my first novel (*Toilet Bowl*) is either published, unpublished, or re-published again as two books (*Meet the Godfreys, Tour de Bathroom*). There were a few edits I wanted to make, the most glaring error was writing that "Sutton's Bay" was located at the "tip of the index finger" on the Michigan hand test. That's way off. I'm not sure how I made this big of a mistake, but it stands out like a sore thumb (or a sore index finger).

But the heart of this decision to unpublish the book off of Amazon was I wanted to fully embrace the offline world of books.

Toilet Bowl is about a family business in the bathroom industry and the whole story takes place in Michigan. So why not keep that theme alive in the publishing process too? Go to Diggypod, a local printer in Tecumseh, Michigan to print the book. Go to all of the local bookstores in Michigan, see if they will add it to their shelves. I'm not looking for the full Kathleen Stocking treatment, but how cool would it be to walk in and see a few copies all around Michigan. I'll put it up on Long Overdue Books too. And then chronicle this whole published to unpublished to published again journey in a series (that may turn into a book) called "Unpublished."

Other projects in the works: I try and publish a new post every Monday on my blog "Medium Rare" hosted on ChicagoNow. I view this blog as my writer's workshop, a place to test out rough drafts. Every chapter in this book began as a Medium Rare blog post.

My next work of fiction is a novel called *Endings* about a writer who can't quite finish his seven book fantasy series. The idea was inspired by how *Game of Thrones* author, George R. R. Martin, suddenly had to speed up his process to keep up with HBO. In *Endings*, the question becomes, "How much control does a writer have over the ending in their own book?"

On Long Overdue Books, you'll see the titles: *The Midwest: As a Foreign Country* and a book on marketing called *Somewhere Between Seth Godin & Gary Vaynerchuk*. I'll write these in serialized form, posting a couple chapters at a time, and I encourage anyone in the Long Overdue Books community to contribute. So, for example, if I list off the 10 best pizza places in Chicago for the Midwest book, and someone reads the chapter and says, "How could you forget Renaldi's?!" that doesn't have to be a rogue comment underneath the article. Why not just make that a new chapter written by them?

I've been writing since first grade. It's part of me. I love writing the way Fabio Picchi loves food (and the city of Florence) or Kobe Bryant loves the game of basketball. And sometimes I'll forget that writing, by itself, is enough. It's easy to get distracted and treat it like a means to an end. Get lost in the questions like, "Did the essay get an A? How many copies did it sell? How many views?" Coming up on age 30, I try not to care about those things as much. I keep writing because I love the process. It's hard work, especially all of the revision stages, but when you see the finished book, it's totally worth it. And then you want to do it all over again.

    I hope to gradually build Long Overdue Books into a place where more writers are getting their stories out there; not rushing through the creative process, not publishing things before they're ready, not chasing views and clicks but embracing the journey; falling in love with the craft over and over again. One story at a time.

www.ingramcontent.com/pod-product-compliance
Lightning Source LLC
Chambersburg PA
CBHW051356290426
44108CB00015B/2032